Praise for *Writing Your Legacy*

"This is the book we've been waiting for: th[illegible] life story, inspired by the master of the art ot guided autobiography, James Birren. Now the fundamental methods of guided autobiography are available to us all." —Harry R. Moody, Ph.D., author of *The Five Stages of the Soul*, retired vice president of AARP, and editor of *Human Values in Aging* newsletter

"*Writing Your Legacy* distills years of experience with guided autobiography's thematic approach to life story writing to help us all more effectively understand and develop our stories. New themes, like building blocks, encourage us to go to the heart of experience and create an authentic, meaningful portrayal of our lives. It's a gem!" —Paulette Stevens, president of Life Story Library Foundation (lifestorylibraryfoundation.org)

"Writing a personal history can be both transformative and daunting. Anyone grappling with how to begin will benefit from insights presented in *Writing Your Legacy*. Writers will learn to avoid a dry chronology by going deeper into themes that guide and shape the evolution of a life like no other." —Kathryn N. Cochran, co-author of *Telling the Stories of Life Through Guided Autobiography Groups*

"When you know it's time to write your life story, you want the right people on your team. As a former history teacher and nonfiction writer, I know the importance of 'getting the story right.' This book will show you how to create a compelling, theme-based life story. It is richly enhanced with specific activities and targeted prompts that make it easier to get more out of your story. I'm a believer in Cheryl and Richard's work." —Jason W. Womack, Med, MA, founder of www.TimeToGetMomentum.com

"*Writing Your Legacy* is your life story in two- to three-page vignettes. I call them mini-memoirs. Cheryl and Richard have written the perfect guide that will lead you through the labyrinth of your deepest memories. Trust them from beginning to end—it's their gift to you." —Leil Lowndes, internationally recognized communications expert and author of several top-selling books, including *Goodbye to Shy* and *How to Talk to Anyone*

"Life experiences happen one after another; memoirists often struggle to place these into a meaningful whole. Cheryl and Richard help show the way. Whether you are writing your own memoir or helping others, this book belongs on your shelf." —Sarah White, president of First Person Productions, 2012–2015, Association of Personal Historians

"There is no greater gift to give your family than the story of your life. Richard and Cheryl's book, *Writing Your Legacy*, is a gift to anyone who wants to write their story and leave it as a legacy. As one who has helped older persons write their stories for thirty-five years, I am grateful for this new creative and helpful guide and look forward to using it." —Richard L. Morgan Ph.D., author of *Remembering Your Story: A Guide to Spiritual Autobiography*

"Has some recent experience primed you to consider writing your life story—passing on a legacy to family and friends? As you consider that possibility, does a huge lump of apprehension swell in your throat? If so, join your colleagues. Among Americans approaching or enjoying retirement years, writing your life story is becoming a national phenomenon. The authors, Mr. Campbell and Dr. Svensson, have helped many people begin the process through guided autobiography groups. Thanks to them, this book is a mighty manual loaded with critical hints, tips, and cautions that morph into a self-guided coach to finish the task—a coach in a book! Herein, they describe a system to assist you in gleaning more material and an easy-to-understand process toward accomplishing that goal." —Mary O'Brien Tyrrell, president of Memoirs, Inc. and author of *Become a Memoirist for Elders: Create a Successful Home Business*

Richard Campbell, M.Ed.
Cheryl Svensson, Ph.D.

Writing YOUR LEGACY

The Step-by-Step Guide to Crafting Your Life Story

Richard Campbell, M.Ed.
Cheryl Svensson, Ph.D.

WritersDigest.com
Cincinnati, Ohio

Published by Writer's Digest Books, an imprint of F+W Media, Inc., 10151 Carver Road, Suite # 200, Blue Ash, OH 45242. (800) 289-0963. First edition.

For more resources for writers, visit www.writersdigest.com.

19 18 17 5 4

Distributed in Canada by Fraser Direct
100 Armstrong Avenue
Georgetown, Ontario, Canada L7G 5S4
Tel: (905) 877-4411

Distributed in the U.K. and Europe by F&W Media International
Brunel House, Newton Abbot, Devon, TQ12 4PU, England
Tel: (+44) 1626-323200, Fax: (+44) 1626-323319
E-mail: postmaster@davidandcharles.co.uk

Distributed in Australia by Capricorn Link
P.O. Box 704, Windsor, NSW 2756 Australia
Tel: (02) 4577-3555

ISBN-13: 978-1-59963-877-5

Edited by Amy Owen and Rachel Randall
Designed by Bethany Rainbolt, Laura Spencer, and Alexis Brown
Production coordinated by Debbie Thomas

DISCLAIMER

Acknowledgments

· RICHARD ·

To my family, friends, and students. Each of you has been a part of my own life story. Thank you. I never could have entered this brave new world of life story writing without the support of Brenda Rogers. When I stepped out of my world, she welcomed me into hers, which quickly became ours. Thank you, Brenda.

· CHERYL ·

I am indebted to my family and friends for their unwavering love and support during the months spent writing this book. I am grateful for Nils-Eric's discerning eye and cogent comments and Chris's graphic design skills. You have all helped, in one way or another, to make this book possible.

· RICHARD AND CHERYL ·

We wish to thank our acquisitions editor, Rachel Randall, for guiding this project from beginning to end, and Amy Owen, who gently led us through the editing stages. We are fortunate to have Rita Rosenkranz as our agent.

Dedications

· RICHARD ·

Long ago, on her first Christmas morning, I promised my niece that I would dedicate my first book to her. Danielle, it took many years, but this is for you. Elle, this is yours as well.

· CHERYL ·

First and foremost, this book is written with love and admiration for Jim Birren, who introduced me to the power of writing and sharing life stories. Without Jim's wisdom, guidance, and ability to ask the right questions, this book would not have been possible. Secondly, I deeply appreciate and value all of my Guided Autobiography students. Without their willingness to write and share the deepest stories of their lives, I would never have become so passionate about the value, nor understood the necessity, of writing life stories.

About the Authors

RICHARD CAMPBELL obtained his M.Ed. (Adult Education) in 2002 and teaches Life Story Writing to continuing education students in Hamilton, Ontario, Canada. He also teaches the *Writing Your Legacy* concepts aboard transatlantic cruise crossings. He is a professional writer who has done freelance work for Canadian newspapers and CBC Radio. He runs his own business, Guided Life Stories.

DR. CHERYL SVENSSON has been involved in the field of aging since she graduated from the first Masters in Gerontology program at USC in 1977 and later completed her Ph.D. at the University of Lund, Sweden. Cheryl works closely with Dr. James Birren, founding Dean of the Davis School of Gerontology at USC, and is the Director of the Birren Center for Autobiographical Studies (www.guidedautobiography.com), an organization dedicated to research and development for older adults to write their life stories.

She currently teaches at USC and has taught Guided Autobiography at UCLA and several universities, libraries, and senior and assisted living centers. For the past five years she has taught a live, interactive Internet webinar training course to teach students worldwide how to become Guided Autobiography instructors.

TABLE OF CONTENTS

Part Two: Building the Walls

Part Three: Trim Work

Foreword

by James E. Birren

Today we live in an impersonal age. New technology has propelled us ever forward, moving from the agricultural age through the industrial age and into the age of information technology. We now have instant communication and information at our fingertips. With this reliance on ever-changing technological advances, we are losing the opportunity to relate to one another face-to-face. Shopping, banking, postal services, etc. are often conducted over the Internet. It is efficient yet impersonal. Seldom do we meet a clerk or bank teller in person but rather connect with them via cyberspace.

Possibly as a backlash from this increasingly impersonal life, more and more people are sitting down to write their memoirs. They understand the absolute necessity of writing down their life story—to prove they existed, that their life mattered, and so that future generations may understand who they were, how they lived, and how they became the parent, grandparent, aunt or uncle, or sibling they became. We make sense of our own lives while leaving our life legacy for posterity.

As each generation moves into adulthood, the past assumes greater significance. Our accumulated life experiences often take us on an unexpected journey in search of answers that may have been ignored for too long. We start compiling our family history. In this age of instant technology, looking backwards can be a giant step forward. Clarity emerges from reflection. We live our lives in the moment, but each step resonates with the learning we have brought with us. The wisdom we gain is a gift that we can share with those who come after us. We can now pass down our life stories to family, friends, and institutions.

Cheryl and Richard have created a compelling work that makes this journey a worthy one. *Writing Your Legacy* is a milestone guide that will stand the test of time. It takes that enormous block of a person's lifetime and breaks it into manageable chunks that can be written in two- to three-page segments. In Guided Autobiography these are called life themes. Cheryl and Richard have taken this concept to a new level by identifying several core legacy themes and adding others that prime our memories and bring meaning to the world we live in. Their book explores new territory worth discovering.

In Part One, the basics of life story writing are examined. Cheryl and Richard set out to understand why we are compelled to tell our stories and how we learn to see ourselves as heroes, and demonstrate how to make our life stories into living legacies. Part Two is all about the legacy themes. From Forks in the Road and Life Goals to Life Values and Cultural Heritage, these legacy themes give substance to the stories. Part Three discusses titling your book, how to enhance your story with images or video, and deciding on a final format.

Writing Your Legacy is a book to be read and used. Readers can expect a compelling life story narrative that closes the gap between wanting to write down their story and actually doing so. This book helps individuals write their life stories and offers themes that help organize those experiences. The themes prime many memories of the past that can be woven into the story of one's life. This book will help many people who wanted to write their life story but have postponed doing so. It breaks new ground.

JAMES E. BIRREN is the co-author of *Guiding Autobiography Groups for Older Adults, Where to Go from Here: Discovering Your Own Life's Wisdom in the Second Half of Your Life*, and *Telling the Stories of Life Through Guided Autobiography Groups*. Dr. Birren received the Distinguished Career

Contribution Award from the Gerontological Society of America in 2002, and he was inducted into the Hall of Fame by the American Society on Aging in 2004. In 2013 the Fielding Graduate University presented The Creative Longevity and Wisdom Lifetime Award to Dr. Birren at a plenary session of the International Conference on Positive Aging in Los Angeles. Jim Birren is an icon in the field of aging.

Introduction

Surveying the Landscape

"All the words I use in my stories can be found in the dictionary—it's just a matter of arranging them into the right sentences." —W. SOMERSET MAUGHAM

W. Somerset Maugham was right—the words can all be found in one place. The real work lies in writing them down and making sense of them. For centuries, writers have pondered the connection between developing their thoughts and capturing them on an empty page. Often a disconnect exists between the two. Writer's block can be the scourge that stops the well-intentioned person from crafting a life story.

Writing Your Legacy will help guide you through the unknowns of getting your life story down on paper. You will not only write about *what* happened and when but also *how* and your feelings associated with specific events and milestones. It is a remarkable reality that as we move forward in our life journey, we do so while looking back. We have one foot in the moment, the other in the past. Perhaps Winston Churchill said it best: "The further backward you can look, the farther you can see." That's what life story writing is about. Thousands of people everywhere are reaching a stage in their lives where they want to slow down, smell the roses, and gaze back on their journey. This book will help you accomplish this while leaving behind a record.

Writing Your Legacy is written from experience. We have taught life story writing to many students in both classroom and online settings. Cheryl has worked for many years with James E. Birren, originator of Guided Autobiography, the life story process out of which legacy writing evolved. She says, "After working closely with hundreds of students from all over the world who have written their life story, I know more than ever the power gained from this process. Through this experience people come to look back over their life, view it in a new perspective, and gain new insights as they begin to understand their life events. This helps them acknowledge where they have been, appreciate where they are now, and plan for the future."

One of the greatest hurdles to writing your life story is where to start. Dozens of books are on the market, and most are organized in the same manner. They instruct aspiring life story writers to begin their narrative when they were born and follow it through until the present moment. The result is a serviceable, year-to-year life account that their family will appreciate owning. But most times the writer never completes her story. The drudgery of moving through a lifetime, year upon year, can be monotonous. The linear progression of events begins to blur into one messy lump of living, scattered across the pages. Those pages often don't reach the end of the first chapter.

Writing Your Legacy is not about writing the chronological events of your life. Rather it is your life story based on *themes*. Each theme focuses on one aspect of your life and opens up old memories. For example, you will first be introduced to a theme called Forks in the Road. Just as the title indicates, it involves recalling a turning point in your life. We encounter hundreds if not thousands of these diversions in the path, and some are more significant than others. With the help of guided prompts, you will choose one significant fork in the road and write a short two- or three-page story. In this book you will find ten core themes, along with many others that can add context and variety to your story.

This Book Is for You If . . .

- you wish to capture and record a life well lived for your children and grandchildren.
- you have survived major life challenges and wish to understand them better.
- you want to write but have never considered yourself a "real" writer.
- you have something to say and would like to be heard.
- you need a project to sustain you during a transition period in your life.
- you simply want to be remembered.

What Is Legacy Writing?

The method for life story writing we propose in this book is different from other methods. If you were to browse through a bookstore or search online for a book, you would find numerous titles related to writing your memoir or telling your life story. Invariably these will follow one pattern: dividing your life into chunks—childhood, adolescence, early adulthood, midlife, and retirement. You will find hundreds of questions: *What is your birth date? What were your parents' names? Where did you go to school? What was your favorite subject? What was your first paying job? When and how did you meet the person you would one day marry?* This method is deeply entrenched in chronological order. It is straightforward but risks being boring and reading more like a genealogical record. It is a linear process that begins at birth and ends in present time. As such, it often fails to capture the spirit of a person's life. Memorable moments do not happen in order, nor do they always happen during key moments such as a graduation, a wedding, a first day on the job, or the day you retired. Instead they may sneak up on you when you least expect them.

Writing your legacy can be compared to building a house—your life story house. First you need to think about the design—who is it for? What is the purpose? Why are you doing it? How should it look? Once you have answered these basic questions and committed yourself to the project, the practical how-to steps must be considered. When will you begin work? Who will help? What tools do you need? How will you stay on schedule? Whether you are laying the first brick or writing the first line of text, you just do it! Once you've gained momentum from planning and have drawn up the blueprints, the rest of the process will grow and evolve as you move forward. You become the hero of your own story because it is your story. Critics will always try to keep you in check as they comment, "That's not how you do it. You should ..." They need to be ignored. Building a custom life story does not require that you follow a rigid template. You can change it as necessary when new information or new desires arise. Likewise, no single right way exists for you to write your life legacy. It will grow and emerge as forgotten memories resurface, resentments are forgiven, and new life lessons are learned. You will find your voice, your style, and your life as you write.

One of the greatest challenges in using the chronological method is choice. Which questions do you answer? How do you link a major early event in your life to an experience that happened much later? For example, how do your initial family relationships impact later ones with the opposite sex? How do you capture these emerging themes? Using the linear approach will cause you to miss such interconnections.

Writing Your Legacy is your life story in themes. You will write short two- to three-page stories on life events revolving around core themes that include:

- Forks in the Road
- My Family, My Self
- The Meaning of Wealth
- My Life's Work
- Self-Image and Well-Being
- The Male-Female Equation
- The End of Life
- From Secular to Spiritual
- My Life Goals
- My Legacy Letter

In this book, each theme has a short introduction followed by customized probing questions. These are designed to help guide you through the writing process while the exercises reinforce this learning. The questions help rekindle old memories. You will write your stories on chosen themes, complete the provided exercises, and, in the process, create your life story. At minimum, using only the initial ten core themes, you will create a 7,000- to 8,000-word legacy story that covers every major aspect of the life you have lived. The process is flexible. Students often choose to expand on the ten themes, writing several pages on each. The probing questions will help you with this. If you choose to add stories from the dozens of other available themes or to create your own themes, your manuscript can later be turned into a book-length project.

How to Use This Book

There are three parts to the book.

PART ONE: LAYING THE FOUNDATION offers an overview of life story writing and covers topics such as getting started, finding your writing voice, being kind to yourself, and recognizing that bad decisions in life can make for very interesting stories. Each chapter in this section includes an exercise that can help reinforce your learning.

PART TWO: BUILDING THE WALLS introduces the ten core legacy themes. Each theme is followed by a short, descriptive excerpt written by one of our students. You can use these stories as guides while writing your own. You may also wish to create your own legacy themes, ones that reflect your unique life experiences; we show you how.

PART THREE: TRIM WORK covers the tasks you'll need to complete once you have written your legacy story. What will the title be? We give you some ideas and help you decide on a title for your story. Perhaps you would like to create your life story using video. That, too, can be done using the legacy themes. Would you like to print your book professionally and gift it to family and friends? We explore the options available. We provide guidelines for sharing your life story writing with friends and neighbors. You will also find an extensive resource list that includes additional exercises to help you with your writing.

A Note on the Exercises

The exercises in Part One are tailored to each chapter. For example, the first chapter reveals why we tell our stories, who reads them, and whom we can rely on for support. The exercise that follows in chapter one elaborates on this. You will find more exercises in Part Two. Those you find relevant to your story are worth completing, as they can add context to your writing.

A Note on the Resources

In the last section you will find additional resource material. This includes a World Events time line if you wish to compare your life progression to historical events dating back to the early twentieth century. You will also find a unique Life Experiences chart divided into sixteen activity lists that serve as memory joggers concerning your experiences. Doing the exercises can help you recall those life events you may not have thought about for years.

Books are written to be read. *Writing Your Legacy* carries an additional responsibility to help you write yours. With this book, we want to share this journey with you. Every book has a life of its own—make this one a part of yours.

Let's get started.

PART ONE

LAYING THE FOUNDATION

In the first part of this book, we provide you with the basic tools for writing your life story. By reading this section and following along with the exercises, you will begin laying the foundation for your narrative.

In **CHAPTER ONE** you will discover the many reasons why you might choose to write your life story. Perhaps you want to leave a legacy for your family, provide insights for increased self-understanding, reconcile the past and resolve old resentments, facilitate personal growth, or assist in the transition from one life stage to another, e.g., from work to retirement. Any one of these motivators is an excellent reason to begin writing today.

In **CHAPTER TWO** you will discover many ways to record the life you've lived. These include autobiography, memoirs (such as coming of age, confessional, celebrity memoir, personal, spiritual, and travel), life review, creative nonfiction, and guided autobiography. Legacy writing serves as a powerful hybrid. It takes the best of many life story styles and merges them into a cohesive and concise thematic method.

In **CHAPTER THREE** we'll get down to business—time to prepare for writing! First, we'll examine how different people learn. This is a key tool that can help you navigate the maze of writing your life story—that is, discovering if you are an auditory, tactile, or visual learner.

You will also learn that sometimes it's easier to start a major writing project than to stick with it. We touch upon a few motivators, including a review of the times when you successfully completed a project (if you did it before, you can do it again!), challenging your internal critics, and being flexible with your goals.

Finally we will discuss how fear can slow down your writing. Some fears include failure, criticism, success, commitment, and more. Letting go of these common fears will help move your stories from ideas to words.

In **CHAPTER FOUR** you will learn that the best writing comes when all five senses are engaged. Who can deny the magic of a story filled with vivid sensory description? You can employ the power of sight, the magic of sound, the pleasure of touch, the savor of taste, and the memory of smell.

In **CHAPTER FIVE** you will recognize some of the difficulties in self-expression and finding your writing voice. Which one is the real you? To discover this, try writing what you know, writing your feelings, writing to your readers, writing with humor, and more.

In **CHAPTER SIX** you will examine viewpoint and discover that you are the hero of your story. You also will learn the challenges involved in playing this role, including humility, power, responsibility, and being on a pedestal. There are several attributes of a hero: conviction, courage, humility, wisdom, and more. By staying true to your heroic tendencies, you stay true to your story.

In **CHAPTER SEVEN** we will discuss interviewing techniques. You may know yourself better than anyone else, but others know you from their own perspectives. Hearing those perspectives can be enlightening and can add depth to your life story. We provide several tips for conducting powerful interviews.

In **CHAPTER EIGHT** you will learn that memory is fleeting and can stay tucked away in the hidden spots of your mind. There are many ways to help you salvage these forgotten experiences. We recommend listening to music from the time period, browsing through old yearbooks, studying old photos, and visiting the area where you grew up, among others.

You will also learn that everyone makes mistakes and has done things they later regret. Dark secrets may haunt us and may also hurt others. You must choose what to write down and what to leave out. You must define your audience. If you are writing for your grandchildren, write accordingly.

In **CHAPTER NINE** you will discover that life story writing can be a form of healing. Time and distance provide a new perspective on painful memories, and writing brings repressed memories to the surface, causing them to dissipate. To help you heal, examine your past, forgive yourself and others, and let it go.

In **CHAPTER TEN** you will learn that humor is often undervalued in life story writing. Yet it allows us to be vulnerable and makes our stories more accessible and understood. We share some valuable techniques for writing with humor: Don't use others for your target practice, use humor for balance, avoid sarcasm, and so on. Life is a combination of light and dark. Be sure to include lots of sunshine—humor makes even a sad story bearable.

In **CHAPTER ELEVEN** you will discover the key factors in building a powerful life story. A few of these include employing the five *W*s (who, what, where, when, and why), deciding on a tone and point of view, showing rather than telling, and avoiding clichés. You will also learn several tips that can facilitate your storytelling and make your writing experience enjoyable and entertaining.

In **CHAPTER TWELVE** we will look into ways to expand your story beyond yourself and reach out to connect with others. We will also discuss how to end your life story when you are still living it.

CHAPTER 1

Preparing the Groundwork

Why Write Your Life Story?

"A man's experiences of life are a book. There was never yet an uninteresting life. Such a thing is an impossibility. Inside of the dullest exterior there is a drama, a comedy, and a tragedy." —MARK TWAIN

Imagine being able to write your life story just two pages at a time. In this book you will learn how to capture the thematic moments in your life: the day you met the most important person in your life, the moment your first child was born, the most unforgettable place you visited, the time you decided, "This is the job for me." *Writing Your Legacy* will help you uncover and write about the most meaningful moments in your life.

We all have a story that belongs to the world—and it's ours to tell. Each of us lives in a world filled with activity. Things happen to us. Things happen because of us. Each day is a scene in a movie focused on us, and we are the leading characters. *Quiet on the set. Action!* We play our roles with style—and quite often we stumble. The times when we trip up or fail become life lessons, and usually we can laugh about them. If nothing else, they make for great stories.

In the oral tradition, stories were told around the dinner table. Generations of ears would listen, and over time these tales slipped into family legend. Sadly most of these retellings would disappear into the mists of time. Nothing was saved. Only the written word will live forever. This is what you can expect from *Writing Your Legacy*. You will:

- **CREATE A POWERFUL LEGACY OF YOUR LIFE STORY AS A GIFT TO FAMILY, FRIENDS, AND COLLEAGUES.** Consider this not only a gift of words but a gift of time. You spend hours creating this once-in-a-lifetime family heirloom. You reach out across the miles to touch the children and grandchildren who live in other places. You share the wisdom of your life experiences: the joys, the successes, the challenges overcome, the legacy you wish to leave behind. You preserve the truth of who you were, your life as lived.
- **PROVIDE INSIGHTS FOR INCREASED SELF-UNDERSTANDING.** Life is a blur. Time for reflection is limited. *Writing Your Legacy* is an oasis of the soul, giving you time to breathe in the moment. It is your opportunity to embrace the life you have lived and to realize that you are part of something much greater. Perhaps Carl Jung says it best: "Your visions will become clear only when you can look into your own heart. Who looks outside, dreams; who looks inside, awakes." This is your time.
- **REASSEMBLE YOUR LIFE-SIZED JIGSAW PUZZLE.** The pieces are scattered across your life in no apparent order. Nothing is unimportant. The most ordinary parts of your life are the very aspects that connect with all mankind. Legacy writing helps put the pieces back together again.
- **RECONCILE YOUR PAST AND RESOLVE OLD RESENTMENTS AND HURTS.** There's no such thing as an easy life. Easy living is momentary. There are bumps and blockades along the way as we nudge up against others. Sometimes we are hurt by those closest to us. The wonder of *life story* is that it comes from the perspective of time. We look back and wonder, *Does it matter so much now?* Or we think, *I may not have*

seen the whole picture back then. Writing Your Legacy gently takes you through this confusing maze of contradictions.

- **RECOGNIZE THAT FAMILY STORIES CAN BE COMPLICATED.** There are often many versions of the truth waiting to be told. Do you want a sibling to tell your story? Your version is the only one you know, and it deserves to be shared.
- **FACILITATE PERSONAL GROWTH AND MOVE FORWARD WITH NEW LIFE GOALS.** We don't live "snapshot" lives that fade with time. Everything moves forward, with each moment becoming a seamless leap into the next. Philosopher Georg Hegel suggested that philosophy can only understand life in hindsight. The same is true with our own lives. Legacy writing helps us reflect on the old. Then we take that information with us as we create new experiences. Past mistakes may hurt, but they can also make us stronger. They can propel us into the unknown with new challenges, new understanding, and new life goals.
- **ASSIST IN THE TRANSITION FROM ONE LIFE STAGE TO ANOTHER, FOR EXAMPLE, FROM WORK TO RETIREMENT.** Someone once said, "Retirement is wonderful if you have two essentials—much to live on and much to live for." Real life is more than just "cause and effect" over and over again. Inevitably the link gets broken. We move from the single life to sharing it with someone special. We start a family. We get downsized. We retire. In each case we regroup, replan, and relive. Legacy writing allows us to rethink this process and to recalibrate our lives through story.
- **GIVE BACK TO THE COMMUNITY THROUGH LOCAL HISTORICAL AND HERITAGE COLLECTIONS.** Your written legacy can become a valuable addition to your community's historical record. Don't overlook the significance of your life story. It will show as many lessons learned and experienced as those of local celebrities.
- **STIMULATE THE BRAIN AS MEMORIES ARE PRIMED BY PROBING QUESTIONS.** As memories recede, they often jumble into one

another. Legacy writing can help sort out time lines and events with probing questions that will lead you to different ways of thinking. These, in turn, can stimulate your mind. Old memories gain new clarity and purpose.

- **PROVIDE A SENSE OF IDENTITY AND ACCEPTANCE TO YOUR DESCENDANTS.** Research has shown that children who know more about their family history have lower anxiety and more self-acceptance. This can be as simple as knowing how their parents met or from what country their grandparents or great-grandparents emigrated. When you write your life story, you are leaving a legacy that will strengthen current and future generations' sense of identity and resilience.

In chapter two, we'll examine why people tell their stories, how they write them, and what lessons can be learned.

Exercise: Surveying the Land

You might have any number of reasons for telling your story. You may feel the need to look back on your life. Perhaps your children or their children have asked you to tell your story. Maybe a friend has encouraged you to tell it all. Review the following questions to help give you more understanding of why you wish to embark on writing your life story. You may wish to use a separate sheet of paper to record your comments.

- Why are you choosing to write your story?
- For whom are you writing?
- Who will be supportive?
- Is there anyone who might not want you to write your story?

CHAPTER 2

Creating the Blueprint

Ways People Tell Their Stories

"You must have control of the authorship of your own identity. The pen that writes your life story must be held in your own hand." —IRENE C. KASSORLA

Your life story is unlike any other, and it can be told in many ways. We've mentioned the oral tradition where grandparents talked of the "good old days" and the "old ways." The children and grandchildren remembered and would later share these life stories with their own offspring. "Grandma was the first in her family to get a college degree." "Grandpa was a Marine." The oral tradition remains an honored part of our heritage and helps connect generations.

There are other ways to remember and record the life you have lived. These methods are important for you to understand since they can serve as reference points in your own learning. Keep in mind that your life stories need not be boxed into any one category.

Autobiography

Autobiography traditionally was the time-honored domain of retired politicians, CEOs, and military leaders. No doubt when you think of autobiographies you imagine tome-length rags-to-riches stories featuring a blend of heroic deeds, controversy, jet-set scandal, and sober reflection. The autobiography was often a linear recording of a life—from birth to old age—with the added depth of time and perspective. It was meant to become part of the historical record. Today the word *autobiography* has become a generic catchall for writing one's life story. Examples of well-known autobiographies include *My Life* by Bill Clinton; *Love, Lucy* by Lucille Ball; and *An Autobiography: The Story of My Experiments with Truth* by Mahatma Gandhi. Many celebrity autobiographies are written by hired professionals. Often these ghostwriters will have their names attached to the story, sometimes in small print on the cover, or they may be acknowledged in the book. Occasionally there is no hint that anyone other than the celebrity was involved, even if a ghostwriter was paid to do the work.

Whereas an autobiography is written by a person who tells his or her own story, a biography is a life story written by someone other than the person whose life is being examined. (An example is *Steve Jobs* by Walter Isaacson.) It is a common perception that a biography will be more objective than an autobiography.

Memoir

"I'm writing my memoir." "I'm taking a class in memoir writing." These ubiquitous kitchen table comments are frequently heard in coffee shops and read on social media. Baby boomers command the marketplace, and they have reached the age where they want to get their life stories down on paper because they have something to say and want others to know. Specifically a memoir takes a central theme and amplifies it into a life story. That theme may be about how poor choices in adolescence have led to tragedy and then resolution. Or perhaps it reveals how drug abuse results in jail time, rehab, and finally a clean life. Or it may tackle a theme of a single mother raising a child. Everything in the story relates to the topic you've chosen.

The memoir can be subdivided into the following more specific categories.

Coming of Age

The precarious high-wire act of adolescence is often performed without a safety net. Many of us have fallen during this time in our lives and thus find common cause in this emotional turmoil. A typical coming-of-age memoir illuminates this often angst-driven journey from childhood to adulthood. Popular examples include *Child Star* by Shirley Temple Black, *I Know Why the Caged Bird Sings* by Maya Angelou, and *Angela's Ashes* by Frank McCourt.

Confessional

The confessional memoirist seeks to reclaim a part of his or her life, one lost through painful experiences and poor choices. Time passes, and from the perspective of distance, the author reaches backwards, trying to make sense of what went wrong, and why. Confessing misdeeds can be cathartic. Often, a reputation needs to be restored, and a tell-all is the first step to redemption. Typical confessional memoirs include *The Confessions of Rick James: Memoirs of a Super Freak* by Rick James, *Confessions of a Dangerous Mind: An Unauthorized Autobiography* by Chuck Barris, and *The Confessions of St. Augustine*, known as the very first published life story, written between 397–400 A.D.

Celebrity

What is it like to be famous? For many of us, it means living vicariously through the eyes and ears of others. How do people cope with being forever in the public eye? Do they think differently? What's an ordinary day like for them? Does it resemble ours? Do they have a magic aura about them? Do they possess a secret to their success and good fortune? Is it all too good to be true? Will they (or have they) come crashing down into mundane reality? Popular celebrity memoirs include *Boy Wonder: My Life in Tights* by

Burt Ward; *I, Rhoda* by Valerie Harper; and *Stories I Only Tell My Friends* by Rob Lowe.

Personal

These memoirs are about us. Personal memoirists may have only one claim to fame—that they are survivors. They have lived their lives as well as possible and have managed to face the challenges along the way. In particular they have dealt with recurring hurdles: disease, poverty, child abuse, alcoholism, or drug addiction. This is the story of how they have coped.

Spiritual

Arguably, all life writing is spiritual. Our words are given reverence as we ponder our fate and try to understand the world in which we live. We long to know our connection to the universe. A spiritual memoir focuses on our transformation as we search for meaning. As such, it can be the most personal of all memoirs. St. Augustine's *Confessions*, written in the fourth century A.D., is considered the first spiritual memoir. Other spiritual memoirs of significance include *The Seven Storey Mountain* by Thomas Merton and *The Spiral Staircase: My Climb Out of Darkness* by Karen Armstrong.

Travel

The travel memoir is self-discovery through journey. It can depict a war veteran who returns to the battlefields of long ago seeking answers and is finally able to forgive himself. It can follow the journey of the restless wanderer savoring the sights, sounds, and tastes of new horizons. Ultimately it is about a central conflict that must be resolved. Often the narrative includes fellow travelers who may have different agendas or different travel perspectives. The common thread in a travel memoir is movement. As the river flows, so, too, does life, forging ahead into the unknown. Popular travel memoirs include *Under the Tuscan Sun* by Frances Mayes and *Eat, Pray, Love* by Elizabeth Gilbert.

Life Reviews

A life review is a therapeutic process developed by gerontologist Dr. Robert Butler, a geriatric psychiatrist, as a means to help older adults deal with unresolved issues before death. It is about understanding and reconciling one's life. Life review looks back chronologically on a person's life and its significant moments with an aim to gain insights and honor wisdom. Structured prompts and questions include: *Tell me when and where you were born. What kind of education did you have? Tell me about your marriage, first job, and when you first left home. Tell me about your career. What have been the successes in your life?* The questions are sequential, from childhood to the present.

Creative Nonfiction

Some life stories do not happen exactly as told. In creative nonfiction, real-life people are sometimes molded into composite characters; specific traits of one character are combined with those of another. The intent is to stay true to a story through simplification. Events may be compressed for better narrative flow, or dialogue between characters may be fictionalized to better capture a true experience. On occasion, often at the beginning of a book, a disclaimer is printed suggesting these alterations. An example is *The Lost Girls* by Jennifer Baggett.

Guided Autobiography

Guided autobiography is based on a small-group process that guides people as they write their life stories. With its emphasis on creating a guided journey through major life themes, it is the Cadillac of life story writing classes. Guided autobiography has a bedrock foundation of theory, practice, and testing. It is a method that has evolved over the past forty years, bringing it to the forefront of current research and life story writing. *Writing Your Legacy* uses this thematic approach for creating the best life story possible.

It serves as a powerful hybrid that measures the ways we have lived our lives and shows us how we can best tell our stories.

Exercise: Building Your Story

This chapter covers the different ways you can write and share your life story. You may choose to write an autobiography or a memoir, conduct a life review, or perhaps compile a collection of creative nonfiction essays. Each structure and approach has its benefits. To identify which method works best for you, consider the following questions.

- Do you want to cover most aspects of your life, including your childhood, adolescence, and adulthood? Consider a form of autobiographical writing.
- Do you wish to focus on a particular theme in your life? This might include your search for happiness, success in business, or overcoming a major health issue. If so, then a memoir might interest you.
- Do you want to reconstruct life scenarios, compressing life events into one singular time frame, and include fictionalized dialogue to enhance your story? You might consider creative nonfiction as a possible solution.
- Do you wish to write a short life story about reconciliation? Perhaps a life review can be conducted.
- Are you intimidated by trying to write large blocks of information and wish to be guided from start to finish? This book will help by breaking large writing blocks into much smaller thematic components. It is a logical extension to guided autobiography, adding clarity and depth.

CHAPTER 3

Laying the First Brick

Preparing to Write Your Life Story

"The secret of getting ahead is getting started."

—MARK TWAIN

In their book *Telling the Stories of Life Through Guided Autobiography Groups*, James E. Birren and Kathryn N. Cochran write, "Like regular exercise, enjoying a cup of tea in the garden, conversing with a trusted confidant, playing a musical instrument, gardening, or spending leisure time in nature, autobiography has healing powers." Psychologist Dr. James W. Pennebaker advocates that writing about your deepest secrets can lead to better emotional and physical health. In his book *Opening Up: The Healing Power of Expressing Emotions*, he writes: "Growing evidence suggests that translating events into language can affect brain and immune function." His studies indicate that writing down very personal thoughts can positively affect your health.

Many of us keep journals. Why do we do this? We may want a sequential record of our lives: what happened each day, the weather, and the people we've met. We may focus our journal entries on family life. Or we might write sporadically, capturing particular moments that are important to us. But more than merely serving as a record of events, many journals reflect tone and feeling. The five senses come into play when entries touch upon the emotions and reactions that surface through our recorded experiences. Often there is a poetic lingering of words. This is why journaling has the potential to grant us insight, and to heal.

And so it is with life story writing. This process offers insight through reflection. We come to know ourselves better. We see past events from a distance, giving them new meaning. "Did I judge myself too harshly?" we may ask. Or we might worry, "Perhaps I was too tough on my family." We put a spotlight on our memories, casting them in a new perspective. It may be as simple as looking back to find the joys you experienced. *I will never forget the day we met. The first time I saw my baby, I cried.* These are profoundly personal observations that go to the heart of life story writing.

What do you remember about the autobiographies, memoirs, and life stories of famous people? Many of us have read numerous books in this genre. We've probably forgotten much of the content, but if you were to look back on those books, you might remember a few things. Was it easy to read? Did you like this person? When you finished the book, you may have thought, *I understand this. The story resonates with me. It offers insight into this person's life and thoughts.* We gain an understanding that we are all interconnected and that we lead lives based on common emotional needs. *We want to make a difference. We want to be respected. We want to love and be loved.* When you look back on your own life story, or when others have read it, the same needs apply.

Here are a few tips to help you leap over the hurdles you may encounter as you start writing. First, you will identify what type of learner you are so that you can incorporate that knowledge into your writing process. Second, you will learn strategies for managing your time and incorporating writing into your busy schedule—the important thing to remember is to commit to writing daily. Third, you will identify a support person who will keep you motivated as you write. Finally, you'll explore some of the underlying fears that might keep you from writing and learn how to conquer them.

Learning to Learn: A Basic Primer

How someone best learns something new is a unique and personal tendency. Most of us have little idea of *how* we learn, but knowledge is leverage. Armed with this information you can better deal with inevitable roadblocks to writing: resistance to starting something new, writer's block, and a fear that you may not have the necessary skills. It will also help you identify a key tool that can help pull you through the maze of writing your life story.

Different Learning Styles

Back in the 1970s, educators and psychologists began to study the way learners acquired information. As a result, many models were proposed, most of which can be found in academic journals. The one best suited for our purposes—writing our life stories—categorizes three types of learners: auditory, tactile or kinesthetic, and visual learners. You are likely one of these. Many of us are dominant in one area but also have secondary strength in another. Research has shown that 60 percent are visual learners, 25 percent are auditory, and 15 percent are tactile. To determine your primary learning style, read the following descriptions and ask yourself if your style of learning matches. Remember that we are simplifying the process—these descriptions will give you a basic indicator only.

- **AUDITORY LEARNER:** You learn best by listening. A lecture will never be wasted on you.
- **TACTILE LEARNER:** You are a touchy-feely learner. You may enjoy doing things for the emotions they cause.
- **VISUAL LEARNER:** Seeing is believing. You process data much like a computer.

How does this help you with your life story writing? If you are an auditory learner, you will recall many life events by listening to the world around you. Perhaps you step outside your home on a sunny spring afternoon and hear the voices of children in the neighborhood. The sound takes you back to the holiday weekends you spent as a child running carefree with your friends.

If you are a tactile learner, memory can be triggered by physical objects in your environment. Let's say you are setting the table and must decide what cutlery to use. You see an old knife, one that you used as a child. You hold it fondly and remember sitting at a kitchen table all those years ago. You used that knife to cut the fat around the steak.

If you are a visual learner, past experiences come alive in an explosion of color and light. Under a rainy twilight sky you drive along Main Street in your town, and the kaleidoscope of neon signs and yellow-vapor streetlights transports you back to another time when you rode in a car down this same street one night as a child. Your parents were in the front seat, and you remember peering over them to catch the view.

Two other sensory systems, smell and taste, both serve as important trigger points for memory and can conjure up dormant details. How many times have you walked by a bakery and recalled the smell of fresh cinnamon rolls—your grandmother's specialty—wafting up from the kitchen and into your bedroom? Or have you ever been eating homemade chicken soup and been reminded of how it tasted when you had a miserable cold and a stuffed-up nose?

Sticking to a Schedule

"I write when I'm inspired, and I see to it that I'm inspired at nine o'clock every morning." —PETER DE VRIES

As you prepare to write your life story, you may wonder: *How do I get started? How do I keep writing?* You may be struggling with the thought that you don't have much to say, that your life is boring, or that you may not have the writing skills you believe are critical. Stop here. Take a breath, and let's go deeper.

You may feel a stirring in your soul, a feeling that now is the time for your story to be told. That is the pure thought that lives in your heart.

However, there is always a counterbalance: On each of your shoulders perches a not-so-pure thought. Meet your internal critics. They do nothing but reinforce negative thinking. "Spend your time more wisely. Do something constructive. You are not a professional writer, and besides, your life story would be dull." We hear these whisperings over and over until they become integrated into our thinking. They nag at us with each new creative start.

This is how you put a stop to them. This is how you turn the critics into your cheerleading squad:

- Look back to other projects you have completed. (They don't have to be about writing.) Do you remember the reasons you considered stopping? Chances are you still moved forward. And when you finished, you were probably quite pleased with your results. So when you ask yourself, "Can I do this?" the answer is "Yes, I can!"
- Keep in mind that your internal critics are nothing more than self-criticism. Challenge them. They can become your biggest supporters. They want this as much as you do—never forget that. Reaffirm your right to move forward as you think, *I will write my life story.*
- Never, ever be afraid to fail. Without failure, we never truly learn.
- Consider flexible goal setting. Make a plan to write something each day. That's it. You don't need a perfect workspace. You don't have to set aside a certain amount of time each day. If you can't devote an hour, a few minutes is fine.
- Break down your project into smaller chunks. Writing on themes is naturally conducive to dividing your project into manageable parts.
- Don't be concerned about grammar. Just get your story down. Later you can revise where needed.
- Do you have the right tools? A computer you can trust? Have you properly backed up your files should your computer crash? Avoid frustration and loss of motivation: Invest in technology that works.

- Create a word count record that includes the date and the number of words you've written. What matters is that each day has a number. It doesn't matter if it's ten words or 500.
- Reward yourself. For each theme you write, treat yourself to something extra. It might be a magazine you normally would not buy, or it might be a few quiet moments of reflection or a stroll in a nearby park.
- Writing your story is not a competition. It is not a race. Those are obstacles you don't need.
- Your life story project is special. There is nothing else quite like it. Feel that pride and nurture it.
- You might want one more cheerleader on your side in addition to the one inside you. Tell a trusted friend about your life story project. Don't discuss it in depth—just ask for his or her continued support.
- Hang around positively minded people. You don't need to discuss your writing with them—just absorb their energy and make it yours.
- Be open to new learning. Go to the library and find memoirs to read that will inspire and inform your own writing.
- Remember that this new experience should be fun. Liken it to a trip you would take as a tourist, visiting the old hotspots of your past. Allow yourself to re-experience the emotions you felt when Grandpa took you to his office and let you play at his big desk or the time you met your first best friend.
- View yourself with positive regard. Psychologist Carl Rogers defined positive regard as a process of acceptance *of you* by other people in your life.
- Imagine forward. Imagine your children or their children reading your life story. Imagine this great gift that you are creating—for them.
- Never forget that no one else can tell your story. Only you have lived it, and it is for you to write.
- Step out of your comfort zone, and let yourself go. Express who you really are without a thought for the consequences. Write from your heart, and the words will flow.

- Collect a handful of motivational quotes, and post them where you can easily see them. Consider these quotes:

"Just keep the hand moving. …" —Natalie Goldberg

"Don't worry about failures, worry about the chances you miss when you don't even try." —Jack Canfield

"Be miserable. Or motivate yourself. Whatever has to be done, it's always your choice." —Wayne Dyer

"Motivation is a fire from within. If someone else tries to light that fire under you, chances are it will burn very briefly." —Stephen R. Covey

That's it. Out of all the recommended motivators, these can work best for you. There is no such thing as a magic bullet motivator. Yes, you can turn off all your communication devices. You can write during the morning if you are a morning person and in the evening if you are a night owl. But these motivators don't always work. With any creative project, you must step out of your comfort zone. Look on this opportunity as a refreshing change of pattern. This alone can reinvigorate your brain, allow it to adapt to new ways of thinking, and, most important, *remember more*. You have lived your greatest life, and you will find new memories resurfacing as you dig deeper into your own world.

After you have stepped out of your comfort zone, you will create a new one, one that involves the day-to-day routine of writing. When that happens, motivation will occur naturally.

Your Support System

Have you ever begun a project and not finished it? We've all been guilty of this at one time or another. Starting something new can be exciting, and often the preparations are simple. You frame out a general concept. You find the time—initially. You claim a space of your own, whether it is the dining room table or a home office. You get your supplies in order and start writing. The first pages come easily. Distractions are ignored. The kids are in school, or maybe they're halfway across the country with lives of their own. That's okay. You're making good time with your writing.

However, there will always be red lights in life, and writers know them well. One day you will be off schedule and will vow to get back to your writing as soon as you can—no later than a couple of days. You're surprised when that time has slipped past—maybe you'll get back to it the next morning. You have reached the wall. You're alone and not writing.

You need a support system: one trusted person who will check in on your writing progress, provide encouragement, and motivate you to keep going. This person should *not* be your spouse or life partner, or a close family member. Why? Because you are writing *your* story, and what you remember may not jive with the memories of those closest to you. Your story is your truth—you don't need an editor or a critic. Instead, an ideal support person could be a best friend, a trusted co-worker, or a mature grandchild. This special person should not be inquisitive about *what* you are writing, only that you *are* writing. Make arrangements to touch base with your support person regularly, a minimum of twice weekly. The contact can be face-to-face, by phone or e-mail, or through texting. The discussion just needs to be consistent and supportive. "How is the writing going?" a support person might ask. If you aren't on track, she might gently reply, "You missed yesterday? I'm sure you'll be back on track before we talk again." This person can be your ticket to a completed life story.

Overcoming Fear

"The cave you fear to enter holds the treasure you seek."

—JOSEPH CAMPBELL

Nothing is as intimidating as staring at a blank computer screen or sheet of paper. Perhaps you've already tried sitting down and committing your life story to paper, but the words and sentences were nowhere to be found. What's stopping you? You know the life you've lived: all the great things, the moments you wanted never to end, and others that were more difficult, the moments you hoped would pass. Maybe you're thinking, *I know too much about myself, and I have too many stories to tell.* Or, conversely, *I haven't led a life nearly interesting enough to put it down on paper.* In either case, where do you begin? Welcome to the Blank Writer's Club.

A Writer's Ten Most Common Fears

How does fear apply to writing? What does it do to us? It seems we can be affected by fear in different ways. You may recognize yourself in some of the following ten mannerisms.

1. **FEAR OF INADEQUACY:** We put ourselves on the line when we write—even if our words are just for ourselves initially. There is permanence in writing. The spoken word can evaporate into nothing, but when those same words are etched into form and substance they can become intimidating. What will others think? What will *you* think? Remember that your life is built on failure. No matter what your standing in life is now, you are here because you failed and learned.
2. **FEAR OF CRITICISM:** Who likes to be criticized? Even constructive criticism sometimes hurts. We usually write our life stories for others, especially family members and successive generations. Therefore we know we are entering the public forum, which always involves risk. What if the writing is weak? What if some of the facts are wrong? What if someone gets left out? What if someone who is included preferred that you hadn't mentioned him or her? To conquer this fear, consider that, for now, this project is yours alone. No one else needs to read it—not yet. Maybe never. Write your life story. Then you can read it, edit it, and decide to share it—or not.
3. **FEAR OF SUCCESS:** You might experience this fear if you have always stayed within your comfort zone with your writing. Perhaps before now you've written just for you, maybe in a journal. In your private writing sessions, words and sentences unfold naturally, and you enjoy the process. But now it's different. This project is meant for others. The stakes are higher. What if they really like it? What if they

want more from you? What if success with this story turns out to be a fluke? Do you really want all of this potential change in your life?

Do not fear success and its possible consequences. Your progress in life thus far is a result of success. Why stop now?

4. **FEAR OF MAKING MISTAKES:** It's easy to stay in a holding pattern, circling around a new project, thinking about it, planning it, researching it, doing everything but the actual writing. You believe your story should have no rough edges, even at the beginning. It all needs to be shiny and perfect. Yes, for you, perfectionism has reared its ugly head. Perfectionists venture into the unknown with great trepidation, if they even start writing at all. They do this because their carefully managed personas are fragile. If this sounds like you, remember that your mistakes only show that you have learned something new. Plus, your rough draft is called "rough" because it's not shiny and perfect. You're supposed to have flaws and mistakes at the beginning. Revision can come later. Just start writing.
5. **FEAR OF COMMITMENT:** Time is a limited resource. Planning a new project often means giving something else up. It also means accepting new responsibility. If you don't currently have balance in your life, tackling your life story and committing to the time and effort it requires will be difficult to accomplish. It can be tempting to say, "I'll do this when the time is right." But the time is now, and it's all you have. As the Nike slogan tells us, "Just do it!"
6. **FEAR OF HAVING NOTHING TO SAY:** This is a fear that can strike any writer, regardless of the project or genre, but when it strikes at a life story writer, the underlying message is usually "My life is not important enough to write about." Only you can overcome this hurdle. In your mind's eye, picture future family members reading, discussing, and learning from your story. Write it for them.
7. **FEAR OF BEING TOO OLD:** You may feel you don't have the strength and energy to write your entire life story. You are never too old to write for an hour a day. If you were, you would not be reading this book. Start by committing to two pages at a time. You might find the words flow easier than you thought.

8. **FEAR OF EXPOSURE:** All writers fear that they may be too revealing in their stories. When we write, we bare our souls and fear what others might "read into" our stories. But everyone has demons, and many of the secrets we consider "shocking" are often very relatable. This is your life as lived—never apologize for it.
9. **FEAR OF TOO MUCH WORK:** You may worry about the time and energy involved in digging through old boxes of photos, calling on long-lost relatives who might add to your memories, or simply sitting for hours at your desk writing. You don't know how this will feel until you start. You may find yourself inspired and energized by writing a story that puts the spotlight on you. One older student in our writing class reported in amazement that she had written long into the night. She was in the flow.
10. **FEAR OF REJECTION:** We all want our writing to be accepted, acknowledged, and acclaimed. However, there is always the risk that some people will not like it. You cannot please everyone, and if you try, your writing will be insipid and lifeless. By succumbing to this fear, you will have failed your true self.

Five Ways to Challenge Your Fears

We all deal with fear in our own way. We avoid it. We confront it. We face it alone or with others. The good news is that fear is often greater in your imagination than in reality. Here are five proven ways to help you get your life story told.

1. **FACE YOUR FEARS:** Easier said than done! How do you know which specific fears are preventing you from writing? You will likely not experience the classic sweaty palms and pounding heart by just thinking of writing. However, you may find that you are delaying the process by busying yourself with other tasks rather than facing that blank page. When you find yourself taking too much time organizing your writing files, compiling mountains of notes, or cleaning

your office, you know you are in the grips of fear. Name your fears, say them out loud, and then allow yourself to move through them as you write your first words. Don't let those fears rule you. Just write!

2. **TAKE IT ONE STEP AT A TIME:** Experiencing fear means you have left the present moment and projected yourself into the future. You might be surrounded by a swirling eddy of negative thoughts. *What will others think? I can't write. I'll never finish this.* Remind yourself that you don't know if your fears will ever be realized. Think of the energy you waste on worrying. Stay in the moment: Focus on writing one word at a time.
3. **CONNECT WITH YOUR INTENDED READERS:** What would it mean to you to have a copy of your mother's or father's life story? How about the story of your grandparents' immigration to this country? We all want to know more about our ancestors' lives—how they became the people they grew into. What were they like as children? What did they leave behind as legacies? Apply this mind-set to your own work. Your life story will be a valuable document for generations to come.
4. **ACCEPT THE POSSIBILITY OF FAILURE:** Yes, maybe you won't live to see the completion of your life story. Maybe no one will take the time to read your story. These are possibilities, but if you face them squarely and move forward in spite of them, you will produce a life story worth telling—and reading. Remember that the only real failure is to not even try.
5. **FIND YOUR ONE AND ONLY:** As we said earlier, find your one true support person who believes in you without reservation. This is the person who is always there for you, who will root for you as you write and stand by you when you need an extra boost of motivation. You need someone who believes in you when your own belief falters.

Greek philosopher Epictetus wrote, "If you wish to be a writer, write." That may be good advice to an aspiring professional writer, but where do you fit in? You just want to write your life story. Novelist Raymond Chandler wrote, "Everything a writer learns about the art or craft of fiction takes just a little away from his need or desire to write at all. In the end he knows all the tricks and has nothing to say." This applies not just to fiction but to any form of writing.

You are different. You have something to say. You are the expert in all things *you*. You know what your childhood was like. You know how your experiences in adolescence profoundly affected the adult you became. Things happen. They happen all the time—when you least expect them. There's no science to life, and so there's no formula to figure it all out. But this is your life story, and writing it to the best of your ability is all you can ask of yourself.

In his book *You Don't Have to Be Famous: How to Write Your Life Story*, Steve Zousmer suggests a unique way to deal with your fear. "Pick something you know you can write without bogging down. It can be an anecdote, an image, a scene, a memory, a description, a joke, a declaration—anything that gets you moving. Before long, probably without realizing it, your writing muscles will loosen. ..."

Fear of the Real Story

There's another barrier to writing, and it happens more with life story writing than with any other form. Sometimes we skirt around a particular life event. We write a highly edited, superficial version of what happened. The description of a traumatic, emotional experience, such as divorce, ends up being less than a page long. It becomes nothing more than a flat, linear narrative.

Consider this powerful description.

> On March 10 of that terrible year, we separated. I left my home for the last time. My life would never be the same. It was like someone had put a gun to my face, pulled the trigger, and taken me out of one life and dumped me into another.

So far, so good. But often that's where the story ends. The reader gets no sense of what the divorce was like for the writer. What actually happened the day he left home? Who was there? What emotions did he feel? Disbelief, anger, fear? The writer moves around the story rather than sinking into it. Why? He is afraid of the truth.

Let's rewrite the scene to add descriptive information that will enhance it.

> On March 10 of that terrible year, Hilary and I separated. We had been married for almost ten years; our daughter Lydia was just turning five. I had taken her to the park that same morning, where she had wrapped her arms around me and whispered, "I love you, Daddy." Had she known something then? Later that afternoon Hilary asked if we could talk. Sure, of course; we did that often. "Let's go out to the deck. Lydia doesn't need to hear this."

Face your fears—write your truth—and you will be rewarded with a life story worth reading.

Exercise: Your Team of Builders

We live our lives surrounded by an ever-changing social network of family, friends, and people you know through various avenues in your life, such as work and common interests. You might be close to some people and know them intimately, while others are simply acquaintances. Envision this social network as a series of circles within each other. Your closest confidants are in the center circle, and the other circles radiate from that point to represent ever more distant people in your life. This network constitutes the main characters in your life story. Who are they? How have they changed over the course of your lifetime? Who is there for you today?

On a separate sheet of paper, write the categories "Childhood," "Adolescence," "Adult Years," and "Present," leaving space under each heading. Then answer the following questions about the different social networks you had or have for each stage in your life.

- **CONFIDANTS:** What strengths did they exhibit? How did they make a difference in my life?

- **PEOPLE WHO HELP:** What strengths did they exhibit? How did they make a difference in my life?
- **FRIENDS:** What strengths did they exhibit? How did they make a difference in my life?
- **ACQUAINTANCES:** What strengths did they exhibit? How did they make a difference in my life?

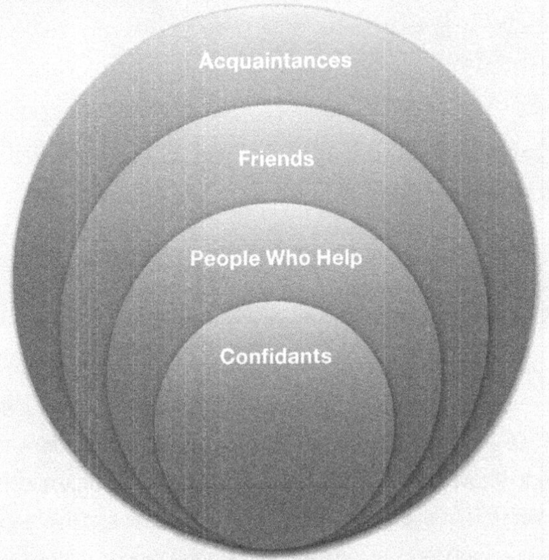

Here are some follow-up questions once you complete this exercise:

- What life stories do these names bring to mind?
- How many people from your childhood remain in your life today?
- Which ones have influenced you the most in terms of who you are today?
- What about those from your adolescence and adult years?

Exercise: Getting the Job Done

Writing is a lonely business. It's just you and the blank page. Sometimes you need all the motivation you can find. But where can you look? Try this checklist to see which motivators might work for you.

- Have you worked on a major project before—and did you complete it?
- Are you afraid of failure with this project?
- Is breaking this project into small units a realistic option?
- Are you willing to write without initial concern over grammar and structure?
- Do you have a good work area with adequate writing tools?
- Are you planning to create a word count sheet to track your daily writing?
- Will you be sharing your life story writing progress with a close friend?
- Are you able to see this project as a labor of love?
- Are you willing to reward yourself as you reach specific writing goals?
- Will you commit to write, even if you do not feel inspired?

These are tough questions. Review your checked-off answers to see what motivational barriers you might be facing. And remember that they serve only as reminders to never give up.

Exercise: Ghosts in the Woodwork

We all experience the fear of failure. As writers, it gives us a sense of foreboding as we stare at the empty page in front of us. How do we fill it with words that matter? How can we write down what seems so simple to think about? One method is an idea proposed by executive coach and author Jason W. Womack in his book *Your Best Just Got Better.* He suggests breaking a task down into fifteen-minute segments. There are ninety-six of these chunks in a day. When you begin your life story project, set your timer and give yourself just fifteen minutes to write. Stay focused. When the time is up, take a break.

Give this idea a try by reviewing the following sentence prompts. Select one, write it down on a blank sheet of paper or type it in a blank document in your word processor, and continue writing on this line of thought for fifteen minutes. Don't stop.

- As a ten-year-old child, I ...
- I'm like my mother/father when I ...
- I become afraid when ...
- Today I want to ...
- My body is ...

Once you have completed your fifteen-minute session, read over what you have just written. If you have the time, go for another fifteen minutes, choosing a different sentence prompt. Putting this fifteen-minute exercise into regular practice is an excellent way to combat those ghosts in the woodwork.

CHAPTER 4

The Big Picture

Perceiving with All the Senses

"All we have to believe is our senses: the tools we use to perceive the world, our sight, our touch, our memory. If they lie to us, then nothing can be trusted."

—NEIL GAIMAN

Sight, sound, touch, taste, smell: These are the secret ingredients to vibrant writing. We use these senses to connect with the world around us. Each day we surround ourselves with an enchanting web of sensual awareness. In our kitchens we see the morning light filtering through the windows, we hear the water running, we feel the penetrating coolness of the fridge as we open its door, we smell the coffee brewing, and we taste the hot, buttered toast. In our shopping malls we see the color collage of stores and kiosks, we hear the upbeat ambient music, we feel the smooth glossiness of the escalator handrail, we smell the antiseptic blandness of climate-controlled air, and we taste the sample eggnog latté handed to us as we pass by the café entrance.

The five senses play major parts in our everyday lives. Each adds context to our experiences: A sunny, cloudless sky can lift a sagging heart, a child's giggle can hold us in a happy moment just a bit longer, and the sweet, drifting smell of fresh-cut grass can transport us back in time, to summers long ago.

In turn, describing our life stories using all five senses brings life to our writing and creates a sense of place for your reader to immerse herself within. When you write your life story, you need to capture the energy perceived by your senses and transform it into words that hum and vibrate. What greater gift to give a reader than to envelope her completely in your life? Here are some ways to do just that.

The Power of Sight

"The question is not what you look at, but what you see." —HENRY DAVID THOREAU

The world is our visual utopia. It is a vast, neutral space in which we live our lives. Visual images bring our thoughts and feelings to life. We wake up to a blue morning sky, one that sends joy into our hearts. We look into the yard with its color splash of flowerbeds ruffled by the summer breeze. We pad quietly across the oak-varnished hallway into the kitchen, stepping gingerly over a black cat named Mildred who sleeps anywhere she chooses. We fill the red kettle with water and set it atop the black-coiled stove burner. The cabinet holds a mishmash of coffee mugs; we choose the coral blue one with *I Love My Grandma* scripted in white letters.

The power of sight is indisputable. Even when our eyes are closed we can imagine color. Our otherworldly dreams are often tempered with the animated colors of reality.

But there is more to sight than just color. Movement is a visual experience. When we attend a play, action is a key ingredient in our engagement and emotional involvement. Actors emote with their facial features, their hands and feet, their posture, their movements. Joy, anger, happiness, and grief are all captured through movement. When a character staggers across the stage, exhausted from battle, we can see his desperation and hopelessness. When a character skips spryly back and forth, we perceive her carefree demeanor. The same is true in real life. We can often see whether someone is listening just by the strain and tilt of a head. No words are necessary. What we see, we can feel.

Your life story will be primarily based on incidents—things that happened to you. Life is perpetually in motion, and everything we do is based on action. More than any other sense, sight dominates. We watch as a girl eagerly leans across the table to smell a freshly baked loaf of bread. She slices a piece, butters it, and tastes it. Her eyes close and her head tilts back slightly as she chews. Describing a scene with visual details adds movement to your narrative and allows others to witness the movie reel running inside your head.

The Resonance of Sound

"In every sound, the hidden silence sleeps."

—DEJAN STOJANOVI, *THE CREATOR*

The impact of sound is present in nearly every life experience you write about. You might recall the time you spent in your high school English class. The teacher was a strict grammarian, and you can still hear the critical tone in his refrain: "Lay or lie? Remember: You *lay* the pencil on a table, but people *lie* in a bed." Even in his quiet classroom you could perceive ambient sound: the girl in the front row dropping her pen on the floor, the boy in front of you clearing his throat as he waited to ask a question, the period bell ringing from the hallway, all overlapped by the continuous low-level din of twenty-five students gathered in a closed space.

Life is a surround-sound experience that may dominate the other senses at times. The high-pitched wail of a siren arrests our attention, especially if it is approaching from behind. An infant screaming on a plane is hard to ignore. Thunder reverberating across a night sky causes us to turn our heads in the direction of the oncoming storm, and, perhaps, to shiver.

But even a sliver of sound—the hooting of an owl at sundown—can create a feeling of timeless wonderment. These small sounds can imbue a sense of reality into our writing, and they are often the most overlooked.

Another unique sound, the human voice, possesses a particular magic. Think of the speakers you have heard. Perhaps your church pastor or high school principal inspired you to reach beyond your comfort zone. How did they accomplish this? Was it only the words? In fact it was a combination of message and delivery. Words alone have their own power, but combine them with passion and elegance and you quickly enter the theater of action. Martin Luther King Jr.'s "I Have a Dream" speech had a rhythmic resonance that imitated marching music. Oration can be a powerful tool, and its foundation is its delivery through sound.

How do you make sound come alive in your writing? Little details are potent: the harmonic rhythms of an FM jazz radio station as you sit in your favorite chair reading, the cadenced *swipe, swipe* of wiper blades batting against the windshield, the roiling winds swooping in off the lake. These sentences are loaded with sound imagery.

The Pleasure of Touch

"Touch has a memory." —JOHN KEATS

Touch is the cradle of all senses. Without it, human beings cannot thrive. For example, orphans left without direct human contact for extended periods of time tend to fall behind in their social development skills. There is even scientific evidence that touch can be healing. It is no surprise, then, that our life experiences usually embrace touch in so many ways. We feel the bear hugs we received from Grandpa, the slap on the back for a job well done, and the firm handshakes after a successful business interview. What about the first time you held hands with the person you would share your life with? How about the feel of waves curling around your feet on a hot summer's day at the beach? Imagine the touch of fear as it surges through your veins like ice water while you walk on stage for your first-ever concert solo.

Touch connects us to the world, and our job is to reflect this connection in our writing. We can do this by bringing touch into every story we write. Use a dictionary of touch-related words such as *brush*, *tickle*, *tap*, *slap*, *pinch*, *press*, *squeeze*, and *twist*.

The Savor of Taste

"The secret of food lies in memory—of thinking and then knowing what the taste of cinnamon or steak is."

—JERRY SALTZ

Taste is perhaps the most narrowly defined sense. The *Oxford English Dictionary* suggests that taste is "the sensation of flavor perceived in the mouth and throat on contact with a substance." This definition brings succulent images to mind: mint chocolate, sparkling wine, barbeque steak, jalapeño peppers, eggnog, and curry. Our taste buds pick up notes of bitterness, saltiness, sweetness, and sourness in everything we taste, and our personal preferences dictate what tastes good and what doesn't.

Think back to your life experiences. What tastes do you recall when you think about the time you visited a terribly expensive restaurant or when you snuck a chocolate chip cookie out of the jar? It's important, too, to move beyond your experiences of food. Can you still taste the briny salt water as it spilled out of your mouth during that long-ago trip to the seashore? What about the grit of desert sand on your lips? Or the taste of blood—metallic and stale—that flooded your mouth after losing your first tooth? These taste memories will add flavor to your life story; use them abundantly.

The Essence of Smell

"Memories, imagination, old sentiments, and associations are more readily reached through the sense of smell than through any other channel."

—OLIVER WENDELL HOLMES, SR.

Our world is the great incubator of smell. From it emerge the thousand scents of Mother Earth: the muskiness of a primal forest, crisp mountain air, and the acrid aroma of a desert gulch. Many of our most vivid memories are of smell. The lush fragrance of bursting lilies can take us back to visits in Aunt Annie's garden. The sizzling scent of a summer barbecue can enhance a warm August evening. The crisp tinge of burning autumn leaves is a harbinger of winter. Change is in the air, and we can sense it.

When you describe your first summer job in a restaurant, you relive the smells: chicken frying on the stoves, breads baking in the ovens, fries sizzling in the vats, coffee wafting in the still air.

When you remember past vacations and trips you experience more smell variations than usual. Traveling to new locales stimulates all the senses, causing them to become more effectively retained in your memory. You can endlessly breathe in the cotton candy-scented carnival you visited as a child. You can still smell the hot blast of jet fuel that stung your nostrils as you walked across the tarmac to your plane. That was the trip when you stepped into the musty world of an English country village after a rainfall. Or was it the exotic spices of a souk in Tangiers that took you away? Think of your travels—near and far—and let the essence of their smells guide your story.

We've discussed the five senses—sight, sound, touch, taste, and smell—and how they add vitality to your life stories. So how do you add these sensory details into your writing? Sometimes it is as easy as setting everything aside for the moment. Take a long look at your surroundings. Where are you now? Do you have your own writing spot tucked away in an alcove? Are you writing in your kitchen? Perhaps you use a picnic table out on your deck. What do you see? If you have a home office, maybe you are surrounded by mahogany cabinets and green file folders. What do you hear? Is there a faint humming from your computer? Birds chirping at the windowsill? What about touch? You feel the gentle tapping rhythm of your fingers flowing across the keyboard. You grip the coffee mug beside you, the moist condensation warming your fingers. You taste and smell a cappuccino with dense foam and cinnamon that tantalizes your mind and body, its aroma floating closer and closer to your lips.

Bring your story to life by describing these five senses. What do you *see* in your story? What *sounds* do you remember? Was the *touch* a memorable one? How so? How would you describe the *taste* of an expensive wine? What about the *smell* of a freshly bathed newborn? Is it the shampoo, the baby powder?

The five senses add depth and sparkle to your words. Use them liberally. Spread them across your story like frosting.

Exercise: Making Your World Come Alive

The five senses—sight, sound, taste, touch, and smell—allow us to interact with the world we live in. They play an important role in your life story writing.

Take a few moments and explore your surroundings. Find one object—whatever is in front of you—to write about, and jot down a paragraph description of what you observe. Try to incorporate all five senses in your description. Which of the five senses do you rely on most? Which is the hardest for you to describe?

CHAPTER 5

Self-Expression

Your Personal Style

"Be yourself. Everyone else is already taken."

—OSCAR WILDE

When we speak, we use different words and phrases for different conversations. We speak one way to our parents, another way to our children, and still another to our closest friends. But when we write, we must find our *authentic* voice and style that resonates with ourselves and with our readers.

This chapter will help you discover your true writing voice, one that rings true with your readers and is an honest reflection of you. Should your story be written in earnest, with a sincere tone? Can it be written playfully, with grace and humor? Let's discover your voice, the one that will distinguish your life story from a sea of other narratives.

Ten Steps to Finding Your Personal Style

1. **WRITE WHAT YOU KNOW.** When you write what you know, you write with authority. You are familiar with your chosen topic. Someone else isn't telling your story—you are doing it yourself.

Imagine if you were to write the story of a person you did not know. Only by learning all about him or her would you be able to master the story. You would have found that person's voice. In the same way, writing what you know will allow you to find comfort in your own skin. Who knows your life story better than you?

2. **WRITE TO YOUR READERS.** For whom are you writing? Yourself? Your children and grandchildren? Future generations? Write as you would talk to them. Otherwise you might sound like someone you are not. If you are aiming to publish your life story, it will become part of the public record, but you need not concern yourself at this point. Just get your story down.
3. **WRITE YOUR FEELINGS.** Expressing your feelings allows you to get to the heart of the story and prevents you from hiding behind clichés and a lexicon of words. You are writing from the essence of the experience, from the belly, if you will, rather than the head. What did that life experience feel like? Does it still bring tears to your eyes? Your readers will want to know that.
4. **WRITE WITH FREEDOM.** Let yourself go when you write. Simply write freely, openly, and without censure. There will always be time to edit later. In order to find your voice, don't try to mimic Steinbeck, Hemingway, or another great author you admire. Simply allow yourself to write—as you, with no strings attached.
5. **WRITE WITH HUMOR.** Even if we do not consider ourselves comedians, we all have a sense of humor. What is yours? Are you a joke teller? Then include jokes in your story. Are you a practical joker? Recount a funny story when the joke was turned on you. We discuss humor writing in more detail in chapter ten.
6. **WRITE YOUR SENSES.** As described in the last chapter, we have five senses: sight, sound, taste, touch, and smell. We each favor some senses over the others; write from your dominant sense perspective. Are you a visual person? Then write how you see the world. Describe the colors and images that capture your attention.
7. **WRITE YOUR INNER SELF.** Who are you? Follow Polonius's advice to Hamlet: "To thine own self be true." Who is your true self? Jot

down a few adjectives or phrases that describe you. When you write as your inner self, your words will flow.

8. **WRITE YOUR TRUTH.** Write your life as you lived it. This is not the time to worry about how your story may impact someone else. Now is the time to simply write what happened, as you perceive it. Staying true to this will allow you to maintain a singular voice throughout—yours.
9. **WRITE YOUR STORIES.** Just as you reminisce and tell stories from your past, write them down. Your stories are the building bricks for your life story. Without our stories, who are we?
10. **WRITE OFTEN.** The more you write, the easier it will become and the better your writing will be. The old adage "practice makes perfect" is a proven fact. Write until it feels like the most natural thing in the world. The only possibility of failure is if you stop.

Staking Your Claim

Another way to uncover your writing voice is to examine what you expect from your readers. What reactions are you looking for? Do you want your readers to like you, sympathize with you, show respect for you? Do you want your writing style to reflect one of these outcomes? Keep in mind that if you try too hard to "make someone like you," you may end up with a flat and uninteresting story. Your best work will come from your desire to let your story tell itself. Worrying about how you are perceived by your readers will result in barriers. There should be no agenda in your message.

In our life story classes a common question always comes up: "How do I write? I'm not a writer." In most cases the concern ends when students have written and read their first story to their classmates. They settle down with the supportive *oohs* and *ahhs* of admiration. What they may have forgotten is that they have written sentences and paragraphs countless times during their lifetime. A life story seems daunting because it spans so many years. Because legacy writing is broken down into thematic segments, the task suddenly becomes manageable. The bits and pieces add up to give you a cohesive whole.

Never forget that your voice has been shaped by your past. It has been honed by years of life experience, good and bad. Your tears, laughter, fears, and joys are all buried in the context of the life you have lived. Your voice is you. If you write consistently with honest intentions, your voice will reflect this. Each life story theme you write will stay true to the narrative path you've chosen. Be honest, be yourself, and it will happen.

Exercise: Home Is Where I Can Be Me

Writers may struggle for years trying to capture their illusive *voice*, the one voice that stands apart from every other. In a sense, they try to capture the essence of who they are and bring that to their writing. It can be a daunting task. There is no easy solution. It just takes practice.

One way to help identify your voice is through free writing. This is a forgiving process that ignores all stylistic conventions. It lets you run free with your pen or keyboard. For this exercise, take a sheet of paper and set your timer for ten minutes. Look at the writing prompt below and let your imagination go. Write a page with your words and sentences. Ignore grammar. If you can't find the next word in your mind, rewrite your last one. Just keep going. Use the following prompt to get started.

"When I get up in the morning…"

Read over what you have just written. Are there any surprises? Do you recognize the voice? That was you speaking. It can serve as your guide as you venture into the art of writing your life story.

CHAPTER 6

The Hero of Your Domain

Viewpoint and Perspective

"I am not always good and noble. I am the hero of this story, but I have my off moments."

—P.G. WODEHOUSE

At first, you might have thought that writing your own story seemed easy. After all, you know yourself best. It should be that simple. You remembered dozens of life moments, vignettes flashed through your mind, and you imagined having enough material for a very large book. Then it began to sink in, and you began to feel overwhelmed. *Where do I start?* you wondered. *What do I include? What doesn't need to be said?*

The answer: You start with yourself. You are the architect, master builder, and owner of your life story house. It's all yours. From beginning to end you have total control over what goes into your story and how to present it. Using the themes in this book will assure you that your life story will be complete—every brick in place, every inch constructed with forethought and skill. These themes will be your safety net. They can help make your life story—and you—shine.

The Challenges of Being a Hero

Before we begin writing in earnest, let's look at the hero of your story—you. There's more to being the hero than being the star. Here are four challenges to being so prominent in your own life story.

The Hero and Humility

Many life stories are written by the World War II generation, who find it difficult being the center of attention. One of their strongest social values is modesty, and they were born and nurtured with the belief that humility shows strength of character. One of their most common concerns is "I would love to tell my story, but I can't imagine anyone being interested in it." What they really mean is they don't like to be the focus of attention. It pushes them beyond their comfort zone. "What will people think?" they might say, worried that others will judge them for being so bold.

Surprisingly, this hurdle is often easy to get past. If shining a spotlight on your story troubles you, look for permission from loved ones. They will remind you that your life story is just one piece of a family puzzle and that it is a gift to future generations. This might be all the assurance you need to proceed. "I will write about my life for my grandchildren. They can learn from my experiences and the world I lived in."

In contrast, much younger people write their life stories, too. People in their twenties and thirties are often comfortable being at center stage. Their challenge is a different one: They may have fewer life experiences in which to show personal growth and change. While they have fully embraced an open society that celebrates full disclosure, as reflected in the desire for transparency in government and business and mirrored by the continued popularity of reality television, younger writers may need to find limits to their self-disclosure. Candor can produce wisdom.

The Hero and Power

As the sole hero of your story, you possess power. You can harness the energy of your life and transform it into a dynamic force. As you work through the themes, you have the chance to flex your writing skills. You control the ebb and flow of your story, taking it through the good times, the challenging times, and, occasionally, the tragic times. Your story, and your depiction of yourself as hero, should have shadings of both light and dark. Lighter moments will be easy to write. However, we are all flawed in some way, and this is where the essence of courage, redemption, and the true story can be found. It is in writing through this darkness that you will become a hero.

The Hero and Responsibility

Being at center stage means that you control the moment. As you work through the life themes, you will begin to sense the wonder of being connected to so many other people. They will live again in your stories, but how do you write about them? What do you tell, and what do you leave out? This is your responsibility. You will understand that all other characters in your life story must remain secondary. They are there to add context and can play off you in good and bad ways. How did a well-respected and much-loved aunt or uncle influence you as a child? If you had a sibling who was unable to deal with addiction challenges, how did this affect you? Always keep in mind that it is not your goal to tell *their* stories. They are in your story because they shared the same life story house at one point in your history. As such, you are not alone. Your responsibility is to show faith in what you write and to portray your characters with empathy—a shared communion of joy and pain.

The Hero on a Pedestal

It can be easy to get carried away when you write about your life. You may have achieved great successes, and your desire to only highlight the good—and to leave out the bad—can be incredibly tempting. You don't have to be famous to fall into this trap. You could be a respected physician, a tenured professor, or the firefighter who saved lives. You could be the local philanthropist who funded community initiatives that nobody else would touch. There are many heroic stories to tell. However, perpetually playing the hero without ever revealing any of your flaws or failures results in bland and uninteresting writing. It won't ring true with your readers. We carry a subconscious belief that most heroes will fall off the pedestal at some point. The real heroics are in getting back up, learning from the fall, and moving forward. That's the stuff great movies are made of. So don't be the hero on a pedestal. Fill your stories with real heroic deeds, but also be yourself. Be courageous enough to admit when you failed and depict the journey you took to redemption. We are all heroes just for surviving life.

Staying True to Your Heroic Self

Who is a hero to you? Is it the soldier who throws himself on a live grenade to protect his comrades? Is it the police officer who confronts and subdues an armed burglar? Or does the word *hero* mean something else to you? Perhaps a hero can be measured for more than just her bravery. There are several ways to define the word. For our purposes these include:

- **CONVICTION:** belief in what you are doing. *Against the advice of family and friends, you set out to establish your own business in a high-risk venture.*
- **COURAGE:** the ability to overcome fear. *In spite of your lifelong fear of public speaking, you joined your local Toastmasters chapter.*
- **HUMILITY:** the quiet dignity of confidence. *You showed grace when your employer told you he should have listened to your advice.*
- **PERSEVERANCE:** choosing to keep going under duress. *You signed up for a 5K race, and even though you were exhausted by the end, you believed you could complete it—and you did.*
- **SELFLESSNESS:** putting others ahead of yourself. *You chose to be the primary breadwinner so that your husband could complete law school.*
- **TOLERANCE:** an attitude of acceptance. *Your new next-door neighbor was the first of his culture to move into your neighborhood. You celebrated his arrival with a container of freshly baked cookies.*
- **WISDOM:** more elegant than knowledge, and assimilated rather than learned. *Your family comes to you for advice since they know you have encountered many challenges during your lifetime and that you wisely know what course of action to take.*

Which of these attributes apply to you? Many of us identify with a few. If you see yourself as a person of conviction, perseverance, and tolerance, these are your heroic tendencies. And as you write through your themes, those attributes you recognize in yourself will become even more evident. You need never use these words in your text, but they should be understood by your readers in the actions you depict and the choices you make in your story. By staying true to your heroic tendencies, you stay true to your story.

Over the course of our lives, we all carry a laundry list of fallibilities. You may be a complainer. You may not be living up to your own expectations. You may procrastinate and never seem to get the big things in life accomplished. You need to ask yourself: *Am I that person today? Have I changed? Is that who I am now?* These negative attributes can show a path to true heroism in your life story. It can chronicle redemption and how you became a stronger person through courageous change. What were those changes? You need to explain how they affected you during that period of time and afterwards. How are you different now? What was the cost of changing? Do those around you, your friends and family, accept the new you? Addressing these questions will help others—and yourself—better understand the heroic context of the life you have lived.

Writing as the Master Builder of Your Life

We've identified the many challenges of being the main character in your story, and you now have a better understanding of your heroic strengths. You might choose *conviction* and *perseverance* as your strongest characteristics. Or perhaps you feel you are best defined through *humility* and *wisdom*. Maybe you've opted for *tolerance*. Meanwhile you may wish to choose which negative attributes you want to include in your story. They may include difficult subject matter such as greed, jealousy, or anger issues. Seeking redemption from these challenges is a heroic journey in itself.

So how do you use this information? How does it fit into your narrative?

The essence of a heroic story is redemption. In his book *The Redemptive Self: Stories Americans Live By*, psychologist Dan P. McAdams writes: "When people tell their life stories, they not only recount the past, but they also project their lives into the future." Art Daily lost his wife and two sons in an accident near Aspen, Colorado. In his book *Out of the Canyon*, he writes about his search for new meaning in life after this devastating loss: "The rest of my life. Do I want to go on? Do I have the spirit, the courage to do this? I don't know yet, but something moves me onward." He adds, "Even in this very early time, when I am in deepest shock, there is a raw spark, a glimmer of faith that is telling me that this is what we do. That we are indomitable beings." Quite simply, most people do not give up, even in the face of terrible adversity and loss.

Perhaps being heroic means nothing more than having the ability to take full responsibility for our own lives. How many times have we heard colleagues and friends blame others for the life they are *forced* to live? "It's not supposed to happen this way." "I've hated that job for thirty years. I can't wait to retire." The world owes us nothing. We don't *deserve* anything. No one dressed in a cape will ever swoop down and rescue us. By writing our life story we come to realize our strengths and weaknesses, our heroism and our shortcomings, and understand fully our own life as lived. This is our deliverance.

Exercise: Super Contractor

It's often difficult to see ourselves as *heroes*. Sure, that's what we'd love others to call us, but we don't usually see a *hero* when we look in the mirror.

Earlier we identified seven ways to define the word *hero*. Review each quality that follows and write down a life experience you remember for each one.

- **CONVICTION:** belief in what you are doing
- **COURAGE:** the ability to overcome your fear
- **HUMILITY:** the quiet dignity of confidence
- **PERSEVERANCE:** choosing to keep going under duress
- **SELFLESSNESS:** putting others ahead of yourself
- **TOLERANCE:** an attitude of acceptance

- **WISDOM:** more elegant than knowledge, and assimilated rather than learned

Can you identify which heroic traits resonate the most for you? You may be surprised to note that there have been many times over the course of your life when one or more of the aspects of heroism has been your guiding force. You may have forgotten the time when you gave up your own career in order to stay home and raise your family. Perhaps you chose to serve your country in the military before settling down. Later you will have the opportunity to list your life experiences. They can be used in many of the themes found in Part Two of this book.

CHAPTER 7

Shared Rooms

Interviewing Others Who Were Along for the Journey

"The art and science of asking questions is the source of all knowledge." —THOMAS BERGER

You've probably heard the African proverb "It takes a village to raise a child." In like manner, it may take a village to gather all the background information for your life story. You may need to interview family members and friends to fill in the holes in your memory as you write about your past. This can be fun as well as enlightening, but keep in mind that the memories of others may be very different from yours. Your mother, your uncle, your son, and your best friend will have their own perspective of you and the events that transpired.

In this chapter we share several interviewing techniques that will help you get the information you are searching for. However, the first questions you must ask yourself are: What am I looking for? Are there gaps in my memory? Perhaps you are writing about your childhood and realize how inadequate your memories are. Or you might be planning to write about a sensitive matter, such as the seemingly incomplete story of how an uncle died long ago. Knowing the specific information you seek will help you frame your interview questions.

Also keep in mind that you can plan the specifics of your interview (e.g., questions, place, time, interviewee), but you cannot plan the responses. You need to be open to whatever comes up during the conversation. Surprises occur, and answers may not be what you were anticipating. For instance, you may be reminiscing with your mom about the time she and your dad first met. You had always heard that it was a blind date and that they went to see a movie. Now she is saying, "I forgot the movie's name, but I'll always remember that your dad was married at the time. I only found out a few days later." Her answer raises many new questions: "How come I never knew?" "Did he get a divorce?" "Do I have any half-siblings I ought to know about?" Knowing the answers, or at least trying to find them, suddenly changes the way you write your life story. It will add context and complexity.

Planning for the Interview

You need to give some thought to the interview process before beginning. Here are a few ideas to keep in mind.

- **PRE-INTERVIEW:** Contact the person you wish to interview, explain that you are writing your life story, and ask if he or she is willing to be interviewed to help you remember. Ideally you want to interview in person so you can gauge physical as well as verbal responses and structure the interview as a conversation rather than a formal affair, but that may not be possible. Geographic distance is always a factor, and not everyone may wish to be interviewed face-to-face. You may need to settle for insights gained during phone conversations.
- **SET GOALS:** Be clear on *why* you are doing the interview. Do you have a specific event or time period in mind on which you need more information? Be sure the interviewee understands what you are looking for and why.
- **PLAN QUESTIONS:** Write down the questions you wish to ask before the interview. Too many questions might prove intimidating, so se-

lect them carefully. Choose time periods and ask open-ended questions that the interviewee can easily fill in with her own memories.

- **USE OPEN-ENDED QUESTIONS:** These are questions that cannot be easily answered with a simple yes or no. A great lead-in question is, "Tell me about …" When you want additional information, say, "Please tell me more."
- **TAKE NOTES OR RECORDINGS:** Ask interviewees for permission to take notes or record their answers. If you record, be as discrete and unobtrusive as possible. Interviewees may become self-conscious and freeze up if a machine is capturing their every word. Get permission to use their information in your life story.
- **LISTEN:** Be fully present as you listen attentively. Don't jump in to ask questions or to make corrections. The interviewee is giving you her time and energy to answer your questions. In response, give her the gift of your complete attention. Let her feel *heard*.
- **UTILIZE SILENCE:** Let silence work for you. Sometimes a person will hesitate before answering a question. Remain still and listen.
- **EXPECT SURPRISES:** You are not necessarily looking for confirmation of past events. The real stories lie in surprise answers. Be prepared for them.
- **THINK AHEAD:** You need to be prepared for the possibility of uncovering some painful memories. How will you respond if there are tears and regrets that come up during the interview? This is where you need to be emotionally present. You can show empathy by being attentive to the person being interviewed. Allow for silence. There is also power in touch. A gentle resting of a hand on another's can be comforting.
- **KEEP MOVING:** If you sense the person does not wish to answer a question, don't prod. Move on to the next one.

Useful Questions to Ask

Most of us are not trained interviewers. When you are looking for information about your own life, there are some specific questions worth considering. Here are a few.

Perceptions

You want to know how the other person has perceived you over the years. If he has known you all of your life, how has his perceptions of you changed? Here are some suggested prompts.

- When I was a child, you thought …
- When I was a teenager, you thought …
- When I was a young adult, you thought …

Hopes and Dreams

These questions are best answered by your caregivers: parents, grandparents, perhaps aunts or uncles. By asking them, you can uncover forgotten talents you might have had as a child. Maybe you had a love for the drums and pounded on everything you could get your hands on. You gave it up and don't know why. Ask the following questions.

- When I was a child, what dreams did you have for me?
- What talents or interests did I possess as a child? As an adolescent?

Missing Information

Ask these questions when you want to fill in your memory gaps. You can be specific and ask what happened on a certain date, or you can ask about someone who was in your life for a short time.

- I remember the family picnic when I was nine years old and you made us leave early because something upset you. That was the last time I remember playing with my cousins. What happened?
- Do you remember my first trip to the hospital for pneumonia? I was too young to remember it.

Family Background

Many families do not tell stories about parents, grandparents, and other relatives to fill in the family history. You may know you are Dutch, but what is the story behind your grandparents' exodus from Holland? Family information might help you understand some of your own behavior and traits. Here are some questions to ask.

- What is one thing about my grandparents that I might not know?
- Were your parents happy when you got married? When you had children?

Last Chance

This is the opportunity for the person you are talking with to add whatever anecdote or story she wants to share with you. It may be an often-repeated one, such as the fact that you always got As in school. But it also may be something you did not know and have never thought to ask.

- Is there anything you've wanted to tell me but haven't?
- If my life story had a title, what might it be?

Always allow the person being interviewed to have the last word. This gives that person some control over the interview. You might be researching for your story, but the other person is a player in this story as well.

Final Steps

Now that you have a more fleshed-out background and possibly new information about your life, how will you use it? First you will need to sit and digest what you have learned. Is it useful? Does it point you in a new direction? Can you use the information to fill in some of the gaps in your writing? Even with all of these new details and anecdotes at your disposal, it is paramount to remember that this is *your* life story. Each of us experiences life from our own unique perspective. When you combine this fact with the distortion of remembered events over many years, you realize that your own truth may be the best one to stick to. Whether you include the new information or not, you have grown from the interview. You have enlarged the perspective of your life.

Exercise: House Guests Welcome

Before interviewing someone for your life story, you need to make a few decisions. This exercise can help identify just what you need to cover during the interviewing process.

1. Whom do you wish to interview?
2. Why do you choose this person?
3. If you focus on particular questions, what theme or part of your life would he or she be categorized under?
4. What questions might you ask?
5. During the interview, occasionally you will hear something that may shock you. It could be an embarrassing family secret or a tragic event. How do you think you would react if that situation arose?
6. What will be your lead-in sentence to begin the interview?
7. How will you end it?

CHAPTER 8

Secrets in the Cellar

Digging Up Old Memories

"Remembrance of things past is not necessarily the remembrance of things as they were." —MARCEL PROUST

Marilu Henner remembers every single moment of her life. She is one of only a few identified people with highly superior autobiographical memory (HSAM) in the United States. In her book *Total Memory Makeover*, she recounts appearing on a television show in 2010 to test her recall ability. She had four minutes to remember events from 1975 and quickly recounted exact sequences from each day selected. By the time she had left the studio she was able to recall in minute detail every day of that year. "Some of the days come up in blocks, such as vacations or the weeks of a particular job. And when I go back to any particular day, I am actually there again in first-person perspective looking out through my eyes and reliving the experience as if it were happening for the first time."

You might feel envious of this ability to remember until you begin to learn firsthand what it is like for someone with HSAM. They can see, hear, and feel everything that happened on a particular day, and this can interfere with their life in the present. Imagine reliving the bad days in your life over and over again. Many of these people wish they could learn to forget.

How Good (or Bad) Is Your Memory?

Unlike those with HSAM, our memories are elusive, often hiding in the netherworld of light and shadow. In fact, we have already forgotten most of our lives.

Techniques exist for pulling these memories into the present, but always remember that truth in story is truth from one perspective. One person's memory of an incident may be different from another's. In fact, this is one of the beautiful things about writing your life story. Your truth is what you remember. Oscar Wilde wrote, "Memory is the diary we all carry about with us." That's good enough.

The bad news is that, unlike Marilu Henner, most of us cannot recall what we did on Wednesday, October 12, 1988. At best we can recall a few incidents and details from that year. "We had our second child." "We lived in an apartment in St. Louis." "I worked for the phone company." Memory is a slippery slope. We try to latch onto it, but too often our grip is tenuous and we find ourselves grasping at thin air.

There are two systems in the brain for storing memories: short-term and long-term memory. Short-term memory is the "working" memory and allows you to hold information for a very short time before you lose it or transfer it to long-term storage. Long-term memory is where we store, organize, and retrieve our memories. Our long-term memories are categorized into explicit (memories that require conscious thought and effort to remember), implicit (memories that do not require conscious recall—rather they are "rote" memories), and autobiographical (episodes in an individual's life and general knowledge of the world).

Your autobiographical memories are what you access when you write your life stories; you will be retrieving memories from your autobiographical memory storage bank. Researchers have discovered an interesting phenomenon involving autobiographical memory. Regardless of our current age, we possess an increased number of memories from adolescence and young adulthood compared to other times in our lives.

This is the time period when you recall the most memories of your life. You may have to work harder to remember events from other periods.

Most people who write their life stories will be older, and that means they may face more challenges in remembering past experiences. Names, dates, and places are often forgotten. Memories may seem less clear—like fog sifting across your mind's eye.

One reason your memories can be inaccurate is that over a lifetime, you have retrieved them time and again, and each time added or subtracted minor details. The original memory has been changed to reflect the newly acquired information. How many times have you recounted a childhood story at a reunion only to be corrected on parts of it? *No, she had pneumonia, not the flu. Miss Murray was our third-grade teacher, not fourth grade.* These comments can intrude on your sense of what really happened. To add more complexity, new information may change your interpretation of a particular event you remember. For example you thought your friend Kathy eloped with John because her father was against the marriage. Later you learn that her father encouraged them to elope because if they didn't, he felt they might never get married. Each time you remember something from long ago, you are recalling your latest memory of it. As time passes, that memory evolves, your understanding deepens, and you remember things differently. The question is (and this becomes more relevant as you age): How can you make memory work for you?

How to Make Memory Work For You

You can try a number of ways to trigger memories of the past. Here are a few suggestions.

- **MUSIC:** Listen to music from the time period you are writing about. If you are trying to recall memories from 1958, research what songs were popular on the radio that year, choose several that are familiar to you, relax in a comfortable chair, and listen to the music. Take notes as your thoughts flow through the music. Where were you the first time you heard the song? Who was with you? What past events surface as you drift away into the music of your past? Jot down your thoughts.

- **PHOTOS:** Browse through old yearbooks. Study the photos, and recall the who, what, where, when, and why of each image. Do you remember the names of your long-ago friends? Do you recognize yourself as a child? Class photos are another trigger source. Each face is a memory, and each person has a history, part of which you shared. Does someone's smile take you back to the day when you first met? Write down notes as ideas and memories come to you.
- **FOODS:** The foods you love can take you on a memorable trip back in time. Think of long-ago family dinners. What constituted a typical evening meal? What was your favorite dish? Do you still eat it? What food did you dislike? Were you forced to eat it? Often certain foods are associated with holidays and special occasions. What is one special food you remember well? Prepare one of the foods from your childhood, and see if it brings back memories.
- **LOCALES:** Do you live near where you grew up? If so, it's time to go back. Drive or walk the streets you lived and played on. Is your house still standing? Has it been renovated? Visit the spots where you and your friends played. What memories surface? Explore the area with your adult eyes. Does it seem smaller or larger than you remember? Are your memories happy ones, or are they mixed? Keep a notepad with you, and write down all your impressions as they arise. If you are unable to physically visit your home, find old photos and envision the area. Try to put yourself back into that time period. If your childhood home was surrounded by trees, visit a park, sit on a bench, and re-create in your mind's eye the area where you lived.

- **READ:** Go to the library and check out some newspapers or magazines from a time in your past you are trying to remember. Just reading the headlines will bring back the important things that were going on in the world at that time. Small-town newspapers are a great source for local happenings. Dig up old letters, journals, or diaries. They may not even be your own—perhaps they belonged to a parent or grandparent—but reading them will bring back memories for you of that time and the people involved. Keep a list of memories that surface.
- **DRAW:** This exercise evokes many long-forgotten memories. Draw the floor plan for the first house you remember living in. Did the front entrance lead into a hall or right into the living room? Where was the sofa? How many bedrooms were there? Which one was yours? Do you remember the wall colors? How about the color of your bedspread? Did it have designs on it? Did the house have just one bathroom? If so, who got to use it first, second, and third? Is there a story about that? Did the house have a garage or carport? Now include the yard surrounding your house. Did it have a fence? What about a set of swings, a pool? Were the neighbors close by? What do you remember about them? Make notes of the memories that arise from this exercise.

When you first begin searching your memory bank, you may uncover memories that are painful. The work of excavating the past may be difficult at times. Remember to pace yourself, to be gentle as you sift through your past. Think of how an archaeologist gently brushes sand from a buried treasure as it is brought to the surface. Examine your past with the same gentle touch. Some memories have been buried for a long time. Your life story belongs to you alone. It is your truth. If you are writing as you honestly remember it, you have honored your memory as well as the tenets of good story writing.

Bringing Light to Dark Memories

"To share your weakness is to make yourself vulnerable; to make yourself vulnerable is to show your strength."

—CRISS JAMI

Writing is communication and requires you to look inward for thoughts and experiences to convey outward to another person, the reader. When you are writing, you should always keep two perspectives in mind: yourself and the reader. Unlike personal journals and diaries where you are free to *dump* your unedited and instantaneous thoughts and emotions because no one else will read them, your life story is usually written for others. The question then becomes: How much do you reveal about yourself? Do you tell it all, the good, the bad, the ugly? Should you try to maintain a pristine image to protect your role as parent, grandparent, and friend?

There is no such thing as a perfect life. Each life has its ups and downs, times of despair, and challenges. As we've said before, a whitewashed life story will come across as insincere and self-serving. But how much should you tell? Most lives, when scratched below the surface, reveal family secrets: abuse, infidelity, depression, despair, jealousy, and loss. This is the area of self-disclosure. Dark stories can change perspectives when set within a complete life story. For example, you may have chosen to include a short section on your divorce, one that happened decades earlier and resulted from an affair you had. Alone, without context, this experience can easily lead to labeling—you may come across as unfaithful and dishonest. But perspectives do change for both you and your readers. That incident happened a long time ago. You see yourself as a stronger person now. That is your new perspective. It will likely be the same for those who know you. People forgive. That's how we survive in our communal society. Your complete life story will show this, and you will stay honest with yourself and others. You have credibility.

Often people feel that they alone hold deep, hidden secrets. In our classes we ask our students to read their stories to one another. Many times, to the absolute surprise of the person sharing a particular family or personal secret, the reaction is not only muted, it is minimal. In their book *Guiding Autobiography Groups for Older Adults*, James E. Birren and Donna E. Deutchman write:

> One aspect of the role of support in personal growth might best be termed the "*Oh*" phenomenon. This is seen when a person comes to guided autobiography with what he or she perceives as a "dark secret," some act or feeling from the past that makes one feel separate and unacceptable. Revelation of this secret in the group is often met with little surprise or judgment. In fact, it is often met with similar revelations or simple acceptance.

No one lives a perfect life. We fail ourselves and others. The real story shows the light at the end of the tunnel. It's how we redeem ourselves. Dark memories may go deep. Forgiveness does not come easily, and there is no scientific solution to manage its outcome. Time, distance, and perspective are needed for healing and growth to occur.

Hidden in the Cellar

"Your shadow self." "Caught between light and shadow." "Knowing your shadow." These phrases pop up continuously in self-help books. What do they mean, and how do they affect your life story writing? In her book *How Did I Get Here?*, Barbara De Angelis describes shadow as "everything in us that is unconscious, undeveloped, rejected, repressed, and denied." The concept derives from the psychology of Carl Jung, who wrote, "It is the face of our own shadow that glowers at us across the Iron Curtain." He meant that we are never far from our shadow, the part of us that is not fully conscious. We have not set it free. As often as not, these shadows are memories that haunt us. When we write about them, we choose to deal with them head on. We write our own tragic episodes. But how far should we go? Do we have the right to tell all? The following is a list of sensitive issues that might arise when thinking back over one's life.

- My reputation is untarnished, and the truth of my actions may hurt.
- I had an affair many years ago.
- My first marriage lasted less than a year, and few people know about it.

- I had an abortion when I was a teenager, and I still think about it.
- I was addicted to alcohol in my twenties.

You may be tempted to ignore these stories or gloss over them because you think it would make your writing easier. However, sometimes half a story can backfire and leave too much room for speculation. For example, if you write, "I had an affair many years ago," likely very few people know about this event. Yet it represents an important part of a life experience—you learned from it and became a better person as a result. So what would you do if this were your experience? Tell the story because it is part of you? Or leave it out because you don't want to be embarrassed or to embarrass someone else?

In deciding what to include or omit in your life story, remember that not every story is available for telling. Some experiences should remain private. You are not writing a deep exposé; you are writing a story that needs balance and that comes with moderation in tone and content. You must be candid—sometimes.

To help decide, ask again, for *whom* are you writing? If this book is for your children and grandchildren, to be read while they are still young, then *write* it accordingly. They do not want too much information. Let them have their illusions of you as a stalwart, loving human being. Part of you is indeed that person. Our reputations are built upon very flimsy perceptions. One negative factor can overrule five positive ones. Your thirty years in a stable and loving marriage can be offset by the one affair you had early on, the one that made your marriage stronger. The affair is what the readers may remember, so perhaps it doesn't need to be mentioned.

You may decide to write everything in your life as it comes up and leave the final editing for later. Writing through the painful memories can have long-lasting positive effects on your life. When you examine a problematic event and write exactly what happened to the best of your recall, it loses its power over you. No longer will you tense up or become anxious when you reflect on that story. You have now stepped away, given yourself the distance and perspective to look at the trauma with new eyes, and forgiven yourself and others. This is catharsis.

Secrets and Repercussions

Telling secrets can have consequences. In her book *The Power of Memoir: How to Write Your Healing Story*, Linda Joy Myers, Ph.D. writes, "Traditionally, writers and artists are the 'different' ones in the world, the ones who dare challenge the family rules and myths, and even those of society." This is not always the case with life story writing. What if you see yourself as *not* so different? What if you are the bedrock of family tradition? Will your decision to write an autobiography or memoir cause friction? It just might. The majority of family and friends will be thrilled—after all, most of them will enjoy shining in the spotlight on occasion and will trust that their best interests will be served in the writing. But occasionally you will run into resistance. The grapevine begins to hum a certain dissonance, and you might narrow it down to old Uncle Ed who does not want the story about his adenoidectomy to get out.

Here are some topics that could be problematic. Imagine how you might address the following situations.

- My mother favored my sister over me.
- My father was an alcoholic.
- I gave up a child for adoption long ago. My children know nothing about this.
- Long ago I was fired at a job for stealing.
- I love giving anonymously to charity and don't want to reveal myself as a donor.

Consider this scenario: "My brother spent time in jail a long time ago but has become a caring, loving husband, father, and community member." Why write about it? It's not your story to tell. At least that's what you might hear from others. But is that true? What if his arrest, conviction, and jail time happened while you were both young adults living at home? Does that not become your story, too? Maybe it destroyed your childhood innocence or created a rift between you and your brother that you have since healed. Do you just ignore the entire event? Life story writers have a way to work with this: They include these potentially hurtful topics in their story if it defines an essential point in their lives.

Discuss the issue with the person involved, in this case, the brother. You might write a draft version for his eyes only and suggest he edit it. Then step back. Does the story still work after his edits? Is there compromise? Will the family relationship remain as before? Most people in similar positions are pleased and relieved to tell their story, as long as they have some control over it.

The Final Step

You have the final word in what material you choose to include in your story and what to leave out. There is no one looking over your shoulder and reminding you that you missed an important part of growing up when you omit your unwanted pregnancy at sixteen. You can write it and then destroy the story. It is the *act* of writing it that is important, not what you do with it later. Editing your life story is the final step in the process, and you still have time to make that decision.

Spiritual teachers remind us that if we must choose between being *right* and being *kind*, to choose kindness. When you are writing about other family members or friends, remember this axiom. We live imperfect lives. So do our children and grandchildren. Perhaps one legacy we can leave them is a story or two of redemption.

Exercise: Memories of Old Homes and Places

Most of our life experiences lie below the surface. Often they remain there for years or decades without us ever thinking about them. Sometimes they just need a little nudge to get them moving again. We can use trigger points to reactivate these dormant memories.

Think about your life as a child, as a teenager, and as a young adult. On a separate sheet of paper, answer the following prompts for each of these memory categories.

- The place where I grew up …
- My house or apartment …
- My health …

- My earliest interests ...
- My favorite and least favorite foods ...
- The music I heard in our house ...
- The radio and/or TV shows ...
- My favorite movies ...
- My first best friend ...
- The things we did together ...

Once you have captured a few old memories, reflect on them for a moment. What feelings do they incur? Are these memories bittersweet, funny, sad, or filled with angst? Remember these feelings when you write, and they will help bring your story to life.

Exercise: Haunted Houses, Hidden Secrets, Good Stories

Family secrets and poor decisions can lead to great stories but only when time has passed, lessons have been learned, and redemption is revealed.

Think back to some of your darkest moments. List a few of these experiences on a separate sheet of paper.

Now take one of your examples and follow up with further questions.

- What events and/or circumstances led you in this direction?
- How did you rewrite your story and find your way back from that dark time in your life?
- Is this a story you wish to share? Are there lessons to be learned? Have you become a stronger and better person because of this experience? Who might benefit from reading this story?

CHAPTER 9

Appraisals and Repairs

Healing Through Writing

"Be yourself. Above all, let who you are, what you are, what you believe, shine through every sentence."

—JOHN JAKES

Writing is healing. You don't need to set out to heal yourself; it happens naturally as you allow yourself to write your truth. In life story writing, you think of the events of your past and write them down. The next step is bringing to the surface the emotions and deep-seated feelings that cling to the events. When you allow yourself to feel like the five-year-old child who was punished time and again for not being perfect, you can now, from the vantage point and distance of time, understand and forgive your parents. Perhaps their own parents also punished them for not being model children. You can let go of the burden of carrying past hurts and move forward, lighter and freer.

This scenario is repeated over and over as you write your life story. All the events of your life will take on a new meaning as you bring them to light. Who you were yesterday is not who you are today, nor is it who you will be tomorrow. Allow yourself to "write through" your life and become fuller, deeper, and more accepting in the process. In doing so you need to remember James Birren's quote from his book *Guiding*

Autobiography Groups for Older Adults: " . . . autobiography is not designed to be used as formal therapy since it is not actively directed toward the cure or amelioration of a disease or a social or emotional problem. It does, however, have therapeutic value as a by-product that occurs naturally." He mentions the healing powers that can manifest through the *reconciliation of long-standing issues.* By looking back at a traumatic part of your life, you will see it from a different perspective. It suddenly may seem less important now.

The Power to Heal

Research shows that writing down your thoughts can be healing. James Pennebaker, in his book *Opening Up: The Healing Power of Expressing Emotions*, writes:

> When people write about major upheavals, they begin to organize and understand them. Writing about the thoughts and feelings of traumas, then, forces individuals to bring together the many facets of overwhelmingly complicated events. Once people can distill complex experiences into more understandable packages, they can begin to move beyond the trauma.

This often happens in our life story classes. Students are first hesitant to share embarrassing personal stories. Invariably they find that their classmates are rarely shocked, and this places the shared information in a new light. *Maybe I'm not alone in this*, they think. They hear stories containing equal candor and depth from classmates and are able to listen with full acceptance. They nod along and think, *It could have happened to me.*

Pennebaker has found that the immune system becomes stronger through disclosure writing. "People who wrote about their deepest thoughts and feelings surrounding traumatic experiences evidenced heightened immune function compared with those who wrote about superficial topics." You may also experience a catharsis after writing about some of your deepest memories.

As we write about difficult life events, we place trust in ourselves. For the first time we may be taking our trauma past the thinking stage and putting it into a more tangible form, i.e., words that we, and possibly others, can read. This can make us vulnerable.

In her book *The Power of Memoir: How to Write Your Healing Story*, Linda Joy Myers, Ph.D. discusses the narrative arc of healing. She writes, "When we need to heal a wound that has been festering, we begin in the chaos of darkness, pain, grief, and anger." She adds, "The arc of healing takes us from pain to awareness and then to a new energy of being who we really are." This process is the psychological journey. Tristine Rainer, in her book *Your Life as Story*, recognizes the mind-body healing connection. "For although therapy is seen as a healing science and autobiography as a literary form, there have always been intimate links between psychotherapy and the restorative powers of personal narrative." It is human nature to understand our place in the world, and to do this we must sometimes place ourselves in the trust of others by sharing our stories with them.

Potholes

James Birren often uses the metaphor of a pothole when describing the tears that sometimes flow when a student shares a painful memory. We may think of a past event and not feel the pain until it has been written and read aloud. Then we feel as if we have slipped into a pothole.

There are psychological risks to writing your life story. The sudden resurgence of long-repressed memories may take you by surprise and rip open old wounds. You may have thought you had moved past that messy divorce or the foreclosure of your dream house. The love you had always wanted from your parents still haunts your psyche. These are topics that are difficult to understand and challenging to write about.

Sometimes we write down our traumatic thoughts and can't let them go. We stew and simmer in our words and feelings. This is a reminder of our investment in that past, painful memory. If this happens to you, keep in mind that energy in any form, even negative, is reaffirmation of life.

Healing happens when you examine your past and present feelings linked to a particular trauma and let them go. What happened? What did you think about it then? What do you think now? Has anything changed? Then ask: Where do I go from here? You can write yourself through the memories and then finally release them.

Write Forward

Never forget that while you are delving into your past, you are at the same time moving forward. You are healing. No matter what you decide to do, be honest with yourself. Don't take yourself where you don't want to go. You can become lost in reflection, with certain memories playing over and over in your mind. You can always stop and move on to another less traumatic life event, or you can decide to ask yourself questions about this one, the one you can't seem to move past. Here are some points to help you when you become stuck.

- The mere act of putting words down on paper forces us to give shape to our thoughts. They give substance to a memory that until now has remained intangible and seemingly out of reach.
- Be mindful of the words you use. How do they make you feel? Were they difficult to write? Do you wonder if they should be deleted?
- Look at the last sentence you wrote. Consider it the end of a paragraph. How would you begin the next one, staying with the theme but refocusing on a new thought? This process might be enough to move you forward.
- Set this memory aside. Begin writing about a different memory—a more positive one. Later you may choose to return to your challenging one. Don't be surprised if you suddenly see it with new eyes. The words might come tumbling out.
- Life always moves forward. You can only go back in your memory. Remember that your life story is a moving journey from past to present to future. You write what happened, and bring those words into the moment, for reference in the future.

Exercise: Home Sweet Home

Writing your personal life story can be therapeutic. It gives you the chance to revisit memories: the good ones that make your heart sing and the not-so-good ones that may still be painful.

We have all overcome tragedy in our lives. Some of us still struggle. Take a few moments and list five life challenges you have faced. Check off whether these have been resolved successfully.

Now choose one of those challenges, and write down just the facts of what happened. Be as specific as possible, and write down only the events of the memory. Read over what you have written, and write down every feeling that wells up inside you in response to this memory. Don't censor your writing. Let the primal feelings of hurt, betrayal, and anger rise to the surface, and write them down. Once you have gone through this exercise, you may feel better. You have purged yourself of pent-up emotions.

It's up to you to decide if any of these challenges will become part of your written life story. If they do, have the issues involved been resolved to your satisfaction? If not, is there anything more you can do? Remember that you are the author of your story, and it is up to you to decide what to keep and what to let go.

CHAPTER 10

Bringing Down the House

Using Humor in Your Writing

"There is a thin line that separates laughter and pain, comedy and tragedy, humor and hurt."

—ERMA BOMBECK

Many life stories are too serious. The autobiographies of past notables often reflect the somberness of the lives they lived, the decisions they made, and the choices taken that affected the world they lived in. Most of us live in a more harmonious world, one that is a wondrous blend of both good and bad. A real life lived is a balance of work and play, successes and failures, joys and tragedies. Focusing only on the serious business can lead to ponderous storytelling. If you use humor you can mention experiences of which you are very proud and you won't come off as being boastful. Your embarrassing moments, told with humor, will reflect your humility.

Twelve Ways to Use Humor in Your Life Story

1. **BE REAL, AND BE YOU:** Don't try to force humor—the effort will show. Your writing will seem stilted and contrived. One way to

find your funny bone is to discover what makes you laugh. What kinds of humor do you like the best? Slapstick? Tongue-in-cheek? Let that translate into your writing.

The humor also needs to reflect your personality. We've all seen and heard serious and grumpy politicians trying to be funny; it just doesn't work. So write as you are. If you're a funny person, let your humor come through naturally. If there is humor in a described situation, it will find its way out.

2. **BE WISE:** Humor is about wisdom. Perhaps Shakespeare said it best in *As You Like It*: "The fool doth think he is wise, but the wise man knows himself to be a fool." In other words, wise people will always realize that the more they know, the less they know. Staying mindful of this will delight your readers. You are giving them permission to just be themselves.
3. **BE SELF-DEPRECATING:** You'll never offend anyone else if you make yourself the butt of the joke. Time and distance from the event you are writing about offers you the latitude to look at what happened and laugh at yourself. You may have tried so hard to make a good first impression that you fell flat on your face. It was not a laughing matter at the time, but now you can see the humor in it. You reveal your vulnerability. As Tristine Rainer writes in *Your Life as Story*, "The best autobiographic humor is when you are the butt of your own jokes."
4. **DON'T USE HUMOR TO INSULT OTHERS:** Other people in your life story aren't suitable for target practice. Aim at yourself instead. It can be tempting to make fun of people as you recount moments in your life. You might be writing about embarrassing or humorous incidents that have been family lore for decades; yet once they appear in writing, the context can change. You may end up looking mean spirited.
5. **TAKE CHARGE:** Using humor puts you in charge of the story, especially if the subject matter is particularly dark. If you can write about horrible things with a touch of humor, your reader will be comfort-

able knowing that neither of you will be overwhelmed. You need to take the lead.

It may be harder to find humor during a sad or difficult time. If you look closely enough and take in a bigger perspective, you may find it. Humor can make a situation bearable.

6. **USE IRONY:** Irony is defined as saying one thing but meaning another, the difference between the appearance of things and the reality. It is used abundantly in our day-to-day lives. We can recognize the following ironic situations. You see a photo of a car smashed into the side of a fast-food restaurant. You think: "Oh, it's a drive-through, too." Or you see a sign directing you to "Hidden Lake." Or you confess that you named your Great Dane "Tiny." Or you see a book titled *The Coming Depression, Revised Edition*. Life is full of these delicious opportunities. Sprinkle them throughout your life story.
7. **PLAY WITH WORDS:** Have fun with words and phrases as you write. If your friend owns a Harley-Davidson bike and you've just bought one that is a less popular or less expensive brand, you might call it your Hardly-Davidson.
8. **FIND THE RIGHT WORD:** Many words just sound funny and form comical images in your mind. Consider these: *befuddle, booby, canoodle, clunker, dither, dorky, fuddy-duddy, kerfuffle, lollygag, nincompoop, skedaddle, titter.* Take note and use others you may think of.
9. **AVOID SARCASM:** A sarcastic remark seems to be praising or complimentary but is actually taunting and harmful. It is often used to put others down and can be difficult to translate well to the written word.
10. **USE CAUTION WITH EXAGGERATION:** We all know the fisherman's story of the "really big one that got away." Each time the story is told, that bass gets bigger and bigger. That is exaggeration, and you should use it wisely. Keep your story true, and don't include people or situations that did not exist. But one form of exaggeration can work nicely for your purposes: when an incident is so over-the-top, so outlandish, that it could not be true. *There must have been a thousand people at my surprise birthday party. Peter was there at his usual*

outrageous best. His polyester pants and pelican-plastered Hawaiian shirt sent off alarm bells—this man needed an intervention. Absurd, yes, but we get the gist of the truth.

11. **EXPLORE THE UPS AND DOWNS WITH HUMOR:** Humor is often about failure. A good friend falls asleep on the job and gets fired. An e-mail meant for a girlfriend is sent accidentally to a former one. These are never funny at the time they occur and are often painful. It is only later that we see the humor. When you tell these stories about yourself, you are revealing your humanness. Yes, we are all in this life together.
12. **USE HUMOR FOR BALANCE:** The art of writing well is about pacing. Life has an uneven tempo, reflected in our everyday reality. Quiet hours are interrupted by singular moments. Routine days and weeks are punctuated by laughter and tears. There is an ebb and flow to the world we live in. Our writing is most successful when it stays in sync with this life flow. Use humor in balance.

Humor generally reflects the truth. It can exaggerate it, distort it, or run over it, but it usually gives you a sense of "I can see that happening to me, too." Bette Midler once wrote: " I never know how much of what I say is true." We have all experienced this on occasion. But as long as you write what you believe to be your truth, you stay true to your story. Let the humor in your writing evolve naturally.

Exercise: Using Humor

Humor provides levity in life. Without it we would not survive long. Fortunately we are surrounded by it. If we have children in our lives, we are blessed with a continuous source of delight. If we live and work in an accepting and safe environment, humor will find us.

You can add humor to many of your stories. These include some of your life experiences that provided little to laugh about. Think of the funerals you attended. Eulogies often contain moments of levity. Humor provides a welcome release of tension. Think of the funny things that you remember, ones that occurred in an environment of fun (playing with the kids, holidays) or in more somber moments (a funeral or misunderstanding). Jot down the five *W*s: the who, what, where, when, and why of the funny events. You will be able to use them later when you begin writing your life story. Take some time now to write down ten funny things that have happened to you.

As you write, think about these two points:

1. Who is the target of the event? Are you comfortable sharing this story with others?
2. Will others relate to the humor of this story as well as you do? How can it be made applicable to your audience at large?

CHAPTER 11

Scaffolding

Building the Story from the Inside Out

"If you can tell stories, create characters, devise incidents, and have sincerity and passion, it doesn't matter a damn how you write."

—W. SOMERSET MAUGHAM

Very few of us can be considered natural-born writers, yet each of us has a story to tell. This chapter will reveal simple ways of making each of your stories more alive and vibrant. We will cover showing vs. telling, varying the length of sentences, finding strong words to replace the exclamation point, and correctly employing basic grammatical rules. We will also discuss simple story structure using conflict and resolution.

Story-Building Elements

There are many ways to build a powerful story. Narrative is about flow. One word leads to a sentence and then to a paragraph, merging next into a chapter and finally into the completed manuscript. Think of a bubbling spring filtering into a brook that meanders through a forest glade into a river and then winds its way down a valley to the ocean. Like the wellspring, a word gains power as it adds to itself. The brook is the sentence; the river, the paragraph; and the ocean is your life story.

Life Story Writing Skill Sets

The five *Ws* from Journalism 101 teach the stripped-down basics of telling a complete story. What happened? Who was there? Where did it happen? When did it happen? Why did it happen? The answers to these basic questions can fill a paragraph or a book, depending on the level of detail you use. Keep the *what, who, where, when*, and *why* in mind as you write.

Voice

Voice is attitude. It is your personality. If you are known as a serious person, that should be reflected in your writing. If you are known for your wit, what better way to honor yourself than by demonstrating it on paper? Are you a "nothing but the basics" storyteller? This stripped-down approach can be an editor's delight.

Tone

"Watch your tone!" How many times have we heard that admonishment as a child? It meant that someone, usually a parent, did not like the way we spoke. It wasn't just the words we used; it was how we expressed them. So how can we, as life story writers, use tone? How can we express in words what we feel in our hearts? How do we take on the responsibility of setting the tone? First, identify your audience and decide how you would like to interact with them. For most of us the audience will be family members, relatives, and friends. Which tone will work for you—and for them? You can choose to be formal, serious, intimate, cynical, or funny. In fact you can use all of these tones. Describing a funeral may be serious but can involve pockets of humor. Revealing a funny moment in life can be shaded with foreshadowing, giving the reader the impression that something bad is about to happen. However, there will always be an overriding story tone, one you will establish in the first few pages. Again, who is your reading audience? If they are your family and friends, write for them. They are your peers. How do they see you? Do they think you are serious, funny, distant, or sad? Keep that in mind while you write. Write to them as you would speak to them.

Point of View

Whose story are you telling? You are writing about your life the way you remember it, and thus you will likely use the first-person point of view (*I* and *me*): "I moved to Palo Alto when I was twenty-seven." The third-person POV (*he, she*) is more removed and distant: "He lived in Palo Alto for nine years." The first person is more intimate. It lets the reader into your world.

Show, Don't Tell

This is telling:

> I was very nervous as I waited at the counter.

This is *showing*:

> When I lifted my trembling hand off the counter, I could see its outline in sweat.

Showing takes you deep into the moment. You are the one lifting your hand off the counter. *Telling* makes for a bland statement. In the first example, you simply tell the reader you are nervous. It may be fact, but it has no color. To add *showing* to your writing, remember to use the five senses (see chapter four). Sight, sound, touch, taste, and smell are reference points that can make your writing more immersive and entertaining.

Here are some examples of showing versus telling, using the five senses.

Sight

TELLING: I saw the bear coming towards me.

SHOWING: The bear rumbled towards me with glistening eyes focused on its dinner.

Sound

TELLING: The explosion was loud.

SHOWING: The sonic boom jolted us awake at 4 A.M.

Touch

TELLING: He held me tightly.

SHOWING: Holding me in his arms made my world a safe one.

Taste

TELLING: The strawberries were fresh and tasted great.

SHOWING: The strawberries tasted like spring and were as fresh as the fleeting breeze that wafted over the fields.

Smell

TELLING: The scent was noxious.

SHOWING: The pungent odor oozed into our nostrils.

Clichés

Editors take glee in crossing out phrases such as "never a dull moment," "a dime a dozen," "the wrong side of the bed," and "my cross to bear." They consider these to be examples of lazy writing. To make your writing *uniquely you*, examine your clichés and reword them. For example, "never a dull moment" can become "a constant frenzy of events," while "a dime a dozen" sounds better as "common and cheap." Try changing "the wrong side of the bed" to "not ready to face the day." How about switching "my cross to bear" with "the troubles with which I must live"? Sometimes clichés work, but they need to be used sparingly.

Simile and Metaphor

Become a gazelle with your writing, swift and sure-footed. Metaphors and similes liven up your writing and add spice to your stories. So, what are they, and how do you use them in your writing?

Similes use the words *like* and *as* to compare two things. Here is an example:

> My life is like a well-worn pair of denim jeans, torn and frayed.

From this sentence, you understand what the writer is telling you: Her life has been well lived.

A metaphor is the more concise cousin of the simile. It can evoke an even more raw comparison with no need for *like* or *as*.

> He was the gopher in our family, always popping up to sniff the terrain.

Notice this sentence has no extraneous words such as *like* or *as*. Consider this metaphor about the same person:

> He was a comet, a flash in the pan, coming on strong and then disappearing into nothingness.

Join these two sentences together—two metaphors—and we have a very strong picture of this individual. "He was the gopher in our family, always popping up to sniff the terrain, then burrowing furtively back into his tunnel." Readers envision a nervous man, forever restless and always on the go. Here is another example.

> My life is a patchwork quilt that often needs airing out.

What a powerful means of giving information to the reader! One can almost see the person being hung out to dry.

Crutch Words

We all have a word we rely on too heavily and repeat too often. It could be a word or phrase that we fall back on over and over again: "Great." "No problem." "Not to worry." You may not even be aware of it, but your readers will pick up on your crutch words and become annoyed. Look over your writing and see if you can identify them. Find the words or phrases you repeat frequently and cut them.

Short Sentences

Limit your sentences to one idea at a time to make your writing less confusing for the reader. Cut out the obvious or redundant words. One rule is to keep many sentences to twenty or fewer words. Sometimes, however, a longer sentence can be more powerful. Ernest Hemingway once wrote: "If I started to write elaborately, or like someone introducing or presenting something, I found that I could cut that scrollwork or ornament out and throw it away and start with the first true simple declarative sentence I had written." Rules are meant to be broken. Do so selectively.

Let's look at an example of an overly wordy sentence:

> All of us lived in Franklin for only a few months before my father was transferred to the far northern outpost of Bristol, a rustic little village that can be found only on detailed regional maps.

Note that there are two points mentioned here. The first is living in Franklin, while the second is the move to Bristol.

Now let's cut these points into two sentences, each reflecting one point: (1) All of us lived in Franklin for only a few months. (2) Then my father was transferred to the far northern outpost of Bristol, a rustic little village that can be found only on detailed regional maps.

> All of us lived in Franklin for only a few months. Then my father was transferred to the far northern outpost of Bristol, a rustic little village that can be found only on detailed regional maps.

Now let's see if there are any redundant words in these two sentences? Can some be deleted or replaced without changing the meaning?

> ~~All of us~~ We lived in Franklin for only ~~a few~~ six months. Then my father was transferred to the ~~far~~ northern outpost of Bristol, a rustic ~~little~~ village ~~that can be~~ found only on detailed regional maps.

The redundant words or phrases are *all of us, a few, far, little*, and *that can be*. Here is the revised version.

> We lived in Franklin for only six months. Then my father was transferred to the northern outpost of Bristol, a rustic village found only on detailed regional maps.

Your goal will always be to tell your story in the most efficient, economical way possible. Your initial writing may be full of redundant words and too many points being made in one sentence. That's not something to worry about now. Get the story written. You can edit later.

Active vs. Passive Voice

When writing in the active voice, the subject of the sentence performs the action:

> Jack hit the ball.

In the passive voice, the target of the action becomes the subject:

> The ball was hit by Jack.

The passive voice usually sounds awkward and wordy. It is wise to use the active voice in most cases.

Use of Adverbs

Adverbs modify verbs, adjectives, and other adverbs. Limit your use of adverbs since they are often redundant and do not add clarity to your writing. A list of frequently misused adverbs includes: *definitely, truly, very,* and *really*. Here's an example of a sentence that does not need the word *definitely*:

> I am definitely going to do it today.

Take out the adverb *definitely*, and the sentence is simple and effective. Notice how it retains its definitive tone:

> I am going to do it today.

Exclamation Marks

Don't use exclamation marks to express shock or surprise. "I was so shocked that I jumped back onto the curb!" Instead, try placing the strongest word at the end. "I jumped back onto the curb in shock." No exclamation mark is needed.

Hints and Tips

- The people in your story may not always be kind, considerate, and caring. They don't have to be, as long as they are interesting and have been a part of your life.
- If there is conflict between two people in your life, you will find a story there.
- Vary the length of your sentences. Keep some short, others longer. This helps to keep the reader focused on your story.

- Each life story segment has a sense of place. Perhaps you are describing your mother's last trip to the hospital. If she was uncomfortable, think of how the setting can reflect that feeling. "The waiting room chairs had once shimmered with a glossy, black sheen. Now they were old and faded. My mother seemed lost in hers."
- Use as many action words as possible in your stories. These are common verbs where motion is implied. Examples include *argued, careened, flipped, gobbled, implemented, motivated, persuaded, scampered, trudged, visualized, and whispered.*
- Stories have a beginning, a middle, and an end, combined with rising action where conflict increases until resolution is found. Not here. You just write your life story as you lived it.

Exercise: Avoiding Clichés

A cliché is a phrase that has become ubiquitous through overuse. Using too many or relying on them too often leads to lazy writing. Once you finish, it's time to do some light cliché editing. Whenever you see one of the following phrases, remove it and substitute your own descriptive words. Take a few minutes to write down ten clichés. Rewrite them in your own words. Try to incorporate similes and metaphors into your rewrites whenever possible.

CLICHÉ: There's *never a dull moment* in our home.
REWRITE: There's always chaos in our house.

CLICHÉ: He is my *knight in shining armor.*
REWRITE: He is my gallant hero.

CLICHÉ: He *got up on the wrong side of the bed* this morning.
REWRITE: He woke up in a foul mood that hovered like a storm cloud all day.

CLICHÉ: The lake was *as smooth as silk.*

REWRITE: The lake was a gleaming mirror.

CLICHÉ: We *nipped that one in the bud.*

REWRITE: We stopped that one just in time.

MORE CLICHÉS

Fit as a fiddle
Scared out of my wits
Nose to the grindstone
Take it with a grain of salt
Get out of my hair
Barking up the wrong tree
My hands are tied
Asleep at the wheel
Pay through the nose
Time to get out of Dodge
Quick as a wink
There's no place like home
Like a duck to water
First and foremost
Give it a rest
Haste makes waste
Sharp as a tack
No laughing matter
All's well that ends well
Leap of faith
Like a bat out of hell
Beat around the bush
Under the weather
Preaching to the choir
Turn over a new leaf
Time will tell
Cat got your tongue?
Time heals all wounds
It was meant to be
No rest for the weary
Thrown to the wolves
All bent out of shape
At the end of my rope
An axe to grind
It's a dog-eat-dog world
On a wing and a prayer
Right on the money
On the cutting edge
Feather in his cap
You can bank on it
Cash cow
Taste of your own medicine
Tried and true
Beaten to a pulp
Piece of cake

CHAPTER 12

Reaching Beyond Yourself

Multiple Perspectives

"Life shrinks or expands in proportion to one's courage."

—ANAÏS NIN

We all have a unique life story to write, yet we are all a part of the vastness of mankind. We are individuals but just one of 7.5 billion human beings living today. How can your small story expand beyond *you* and connect with others?

Each of us is a one-of-a-kind, never-to-be-duplicated person. Our genetic makeup is different from all others, and this distinction is mirrored in our life experiences. However, our stories and experiences transcend the individual and resonate with others in myriad ways. Here are some things you can consider to broaden your life story and identify with others.

- **UNDERSTAND FEELINGS ARE UNIVERSAL:** All humans feel fear, love, hunger, and joy. When you include your feelings in your writing, you are reaching out to all others who have feared, loved, hungered, and experienced joy as well. Our emotions go beyond gender, culture, race, and age, and branch out to connect with all others who have shared similar sensations.

- **DESCRIBE MILIEU:** Enhance the context of your story by adding details of place, atmosphere, and landscape. If you grew up on a farm, add those visual memories of the rural area where you lived. Was it the flat, never-ending plains of Kansas? Or a small farming community dotted with the lakes of Minnesota? In contrast, if you grew up in Toronto, your description of the subways and taxis, the clang and clamor of car horns and sirens, will bring your story to life for other city dwellers. You will touch others with your memories of place.
- **IDENTIFY A HISTORICAL PERIOD:** In what era does your life story take place? Are you one of the "Greatest Generation" members from the World War II years? What was it like before color TVs, computers, and fast food? Maybe you are a Baby Boomer who grew up during the prosperous 1950s or in the "make love not war" hippie days of the 1960s. Read old newspapers and magazines of the period to refresh your memory, and then add anecdotes to your story to connect your life to others who will remember those times as well. Consider the momentous events that have affected everyone—the bombing of Pearl Harbor, Kennedy's assassination, or Martin Luther King's "I Have a Dream" speech. When you add these into your stories, you establish a time line and make connections to future generations.
- **STEP BACK AND DETACH:** Look at your life from a distance. Try to become a character in your own life story. For instance, imagine yourself as the young twenty-two-year-old mother, alone and away from home with a newborn while her husband is in the military. Writing from a place of motherhood alone with a baby connects your story with all women in all periods and places in time who shared similar circumstances. As you write, keep in mind these questions: *Is this interesting for me to read? Would I read it if it was about someone else?*
- **FOCUS ON FAMILY:** Write with humor and understanding about others who have influenced and touched you along your life's journey. Adult children, when they read your story, will be looking for their own name to pop up. They want to know what you thought of them as children, teens, and adults. What were your feelings when

they were born? Comment on your family and friends in your life story. After all, who would you be today without them in your life? This makes the story bigger than you. Generations to come will one day read your story and know you for the first time through your words. Keep in mind as you write that you are reaching out to future descendants.

Using these techniques can greatly enhance your story, stamping it with context and time. This allows others to see their own lives through your experiences and your words.

Ending Your Life Story

Your life story is still being unveiled as you write. You will continue to grow, change, and learn each day of your life. How do you end your story while you are still midstream? Here are some ideas to consider when you bring your life story to a close.

Re-examine Your Intent

Go back to the first question we posed before you even began to write: *Why are you writing your life story?* Did you decide to leave a chronological, historical account of your life? If so, you will be finished with your life story when you reach your current age. Did you want to leave a written record of your thoughts, hopes, and dreams? If this is the case, when you have finished this record you will feel a sense of completion and a natural ending. Have you fulfilled the purpose you began with when you started writing?

Look for More Themes

If you write on the core life themes and beyond as we present them in this book (see Part Two), you will feel a sense of completion when the questions no longer reach out and pull you in. When no new memories arise in response to the themes on family, money, or career, then you are done. You have written your life story.

Assess Your Enthusiasm

You never know when fatigue will strike, but you will most likely reach a point where you are simply tired of writing about your life. You will feel ready to leave the past behind and get on with the day-to-day living of your life. The future will excite you. You will feel as if you've been there, done that. Now it's time to move on.

Look for Patterns

Once you have written stories on a number of themes, you may see a pattern emerge. Is there an undercurrent of love, loss, and rebirth that threads through your life? Maybe you feel that luck and circumstance have played the most significant part in your life; you just happened to be in the right place at the right time to get your dream job and meet your soul mate. Once you see the pattern, you will know how to end your story and bring the theme of your life full circle. One of our students recognized a pattern when her stories about family, spirituality, and death all focused on one overarching theme, forgiveness. She ended her life story with a powerful reflection on this.

Trust Your Intuition

You will simply *know* when and how to end this chapter in your life story. Maybe a poem or song refrain will begin to play in your mind. Your ending does not need to be dramatic or climactic. After all, your life is not over. You still have chapters to write another time.

Deciding on an Ending

It is often difficult to know how to end your life story. One of the most powerful techniques is to read other memoirs. How did they end? Some tell the story in reverse, beginning with the end and ending with the beginning. Many memoirs will give you insights into your own writing as well as how to end your story. Here are some ideas.

1. Choose one of your favorite childhood fairy tales or a movie and rewrite the ending. Have fun with this and play with how the story might end.
2. Now that you are warmed up, sit down and write the ending to your story. Keep in mind that you are *playing* and that nothing you write needs to be kept or shown to anyone else. You may choose to write two or three different endings. Put them aside and review them at a later date. You can then read them with fresh eyes and decide what you wish to keep.

Exercise: Finishing Touches

This exercise will help you step outside yourself and understand and write from another person's perspective. It will take the "me" out of your story and allow you to make connections with others, both psychologically and in your writing.

1. Choose a time from your childhood and write about an experience that you remember well. It could have been your very first vacation or first day of school. Whatever the memory, be certain you recall it completely. Then write down the anecdote, including as many details as you remember.
2. Now take the same incident you wrote about the first time and write it from the third-person perspective. In other words, you will be reporting what happened using the *he* and *she* pronouns.
3. Finally, choose someone else who was present and write the same story from his or her point of view. You will be getting into the mind of someone else and stepping away from "me."

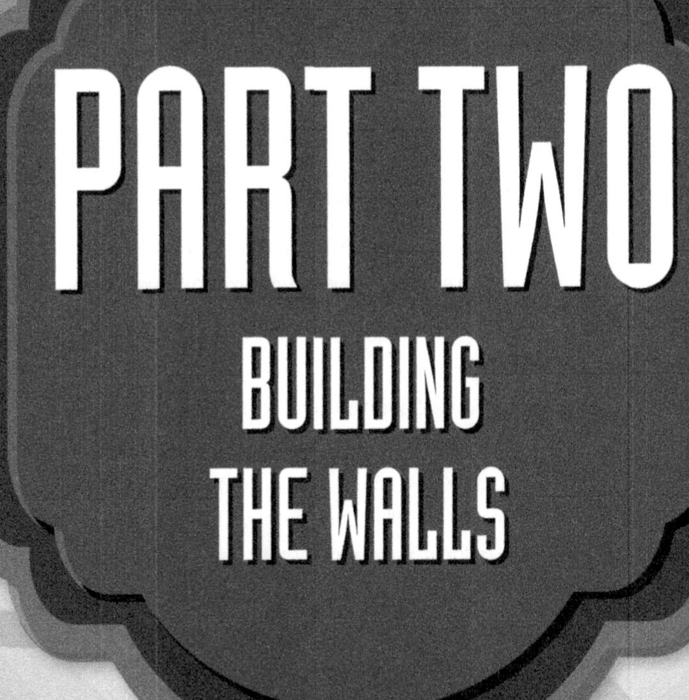

PART TWO

BUILDING THE WALLS

You are now entering the very heart of *Writing Your Legacy*, in which you will learn all about legacy themes and how they can make life story writing manageable and fun. Writing with themes accomplishes four goals.

1. It keeps you focused on one aspect of your life.
2. It allows you to keep to a two- to three-page format, which prevents you from becoming overwhelmed by the length of your life story and helps you focus on the essence of the stories rather than getting bogged down with details.
3. It guides you through your life story in a logical sequence.
4. It introduces key points in your life within a guided structure.

In this section, you will begin writing on the ten primary legacy themes. You will write two- to three-page stories on each theme, starting with "Forks in the Road" and ending with "My Legacy Letter." When you combine all your stories into a cohesive whole, your life story will total between 7,000–8,000 words. The core legacy themes are:

- Forks in the Road
- My Family, My Self
- The Meaning of Wealth
- My Life's Work
- Self-Image and Well-Being
- The Male-Female Equation
- The End of Life
- From Secular to Spiritual
- My Life Goals
- My Legacy Letter

We suggest you write in the order in which the themes are presented. Each theme represents a basic aspect of life that is important to all people, regardless of race, culture, or gender. They proceed from the general to the more profound and specific aspects of your life.

Probing questions accompany each theme and are meant to help you access your memory bank and reveal the treasure of your life stories. Don't answer each question; rather let the questions sit with you for a time until one speaks to you and compels you to write. Write two pages and put it aside. At this stage the goal is simply to begin writing. Title each of your stories so that you will better recall what you wrote when it comes time to organize all of them into one document. You can always change the titles later if you choose.

What follows are the ten themes, each including a sample story excerpt from one of our students. These have been shortened to better fit the framework of this book. Remember that they serve as guidelines and examples only—you can write your story any way you wish.

CHAPTER 13

Legacy Theme 1

Forks in the Road

"When you come to a fork in the road, take it."

—YOGI BERRA

Yogi Berra meant that life is full of choices and that we need to make them. We need to keep moving forward. Your life is filled with turning points. These are the times when you take big or small steps forward. They can be your "a-ha" moments, when new understanding leads to change in the way you do something. They can also offer new perspectives: The day you first fell in love was the day you learned what joy could do to the body and soul. It might have been the phone call that offered the job you'd worked so hard to get. Or you may have taken a trip abroad that forever changed your outlook on life. Possibly you read a book that opened your eyes to new ways of seeing. Each of us has our own unique turning points. Major ones such as graduation, marriage, or death of a loved one are common. Less obvious ones, such as making a new friend who introduces you to the joys of biking, may also have an impact greater than expected. All of them change the flow of our lives in some way.

Probing Questions

Take time to review the following questions. Each serves as a clarifying point that dips into your mind's recesses and helps you access long-forgotten memories. Some questions will resonate more than others. Allow one or two of them to serve as the basis for your thematic story or lead you to other observations that can power the narrative. Keep in mind that they are just guidelines.

1. As a child, turning points are often the result of our parents' choices. Was there a fork in the road that may have changed the course of your life? What were the circumstances?
2. Education often opens doors and new opportunities for us. Was going to school a big step for you? Was school a haven or a hell for you?
3. Significant people in our lives affect us in many ways. What people most influenced your "fork in the road" experiences? Were they your parents, relatives, friends, or teachers?
4. Our life is a mix of events that are out of our control or that we may instigate. Did the many changes you have experienced in life happen to you? Or did you choose the road to take? Do you see a pattern in your life?
5. Change can result when a turning point is reached. Do you regard most of your "fork in the road" experiences as positive? Did any of the negative ones become positive after the fact?
6. Often when change and transition come too quickly in our lives we try to hold onto the past. What change did you struggle against? How did it turn out?
7. We may not always choose the "right" road when we are faced with options. Have you ever made the "wrong" choice? What happened? Could you change it? Do you have any regrets?
8. Was there a change in your immediate family, such as a death, divorce, or bankruptcy, that caused a major disruption in your life?

9. Natural disasters can wreak havoc in our lives. Were you ever impacted by a tornado? Hurricane? Flood? Earthquake? Other natural disaster?
10. It is often said that life is change. Looking back on your life, have you developed an attitude towards change that helps you cope with the uncertainties of life? Do you welcome change or try to hold onto the past?

Student Excerpt: Forks in the Road

Moving from one location to another, whether through our own decision or chosen for us, is often the subject for this theme. Here is an excerpt from one such story by Ruth McCully that shows how impactful this can be on one's life.

> Sometimes you find yourself in a place, a town, a city, or a part of the country, and you know deep in your core that you are home. That is how it is with me. I am a New England Girl. When I am in New England, I am at peace, and deep in my heart's core I know I am home. I belong here. It is a good feeling.
>
> I was born in Boston and raised in a small town, Norwood, Massachusetts. Some would call it a sheltered life. I call it idyllic, safe, and home. We lived on Everett Avenue, a street where each house was different, two stories and old, but not very old. I walked everywhere. I walked to Winslow Elementary School and walked home to have lunch with my brothers and father. We walked to the library, to church and to the movies. We could walk downtown, to the playground, to the municipal swimming pool and to the hospital. Sometimes, my mother would take us all food shopping at the Star Market, and we would walk there and back, carting our groceries in my brother's red wagon.
>
> We played with the kids in the neighborhood. I loved the seasons and the changes that came with them. When it snowed, we would go to the Bond Street playground for sledding, and we could sled nonstop for several blocks through the park from Washington Street to Main Street.

When I was twelve, my grandfather passed away and my father went to Florida to be with him before he died. My father was so taken with Florida, and it was all he talked about—the weather, no need for winter clothes, and the lower cost of living. My father announced that after the first of the year, he was leaving for Florida and we were all moving to Florida. I was stunned. My mother was shocked.

In Florida, I found myself to be a fish out of water. Florida was flat, always sunny and seasonless. The schools were so behind that I was enrolled in both eighth grade and ninth grade classes. The girls were so advanced that I felt lost. Just as plants mature faster in the tropics, so do the girls. I was so behind in both physical and emotional development. I was still a young girl in so many ways, and I knew it.

—Ruth McCully

Exercises: Forks in the Road

1. FREEWRITING: This is your first writing assignment, and you may feel a bit apprehensive as you stare at the blank page. This freewriting exercise will help you get over the hurdle of stage fright. It is exactly as the name implies: Write freely for ten minutes. Write whatever comes to mind without giving thought to spelling, grammar, the subject, or any other thoughts that bubble up when you sit down to write. Write your thoughts exactly as they arise in your mind. If you get stuck, keep rewriting the last word you wrote until another word comes to you. It is most important to simply keep writing and not stop. When the ten minutes are up, put this writing aside and move on to the next exercise.

2. LIFELINE: This first legacy theme examines the turning points in your life. You will be looking at a road map of your life. Was there a side road that your family took when you were a child that moved you off course? Which road did you take when you graduated from high school, and why? This is an exercise to help you remember some of the major changes in your life course and provide a visual map of your life.

- You will need paper, pen or pencil, and a ruler to create your lifeline.
- Turn your paper so it is in landscape orientation and draw a line across the middle from left to right.
- This line represents your chronological lifeline. Label the leftmost point of the line with "Birth." Then mark off five-year increments and stop at the age you think you will live to.
- The vertical axis represents your level of satisfaction with the events. Mark the area above the lifeline with a plus sign, and place a minus sign below the lifeline to indicate the highs and lows of each event.
- Sit quietly and review the highs and lows of your life. On a separate sheet of paper, make a list of the events. Your list may include starting school, getting married, finding a new job, undertaking a major move, and so on. Rank each event from one to ten, with one as very low and ten as the highest level of satisfaction.
- Depending on your age, generate twenty to thirty events. If you are in your twenties, you will naturally have fewer major life experiences than someone who is eighty years old.
- Chart these events on your graph with a dot that corresponds to the age and the level of satisfaction you experienced with each incident.
- Connect the dots to create a visual picture of your life course.

These highs and lows of life have created you. Often the low points have moved you to growth and onward to new highs in your life course.

Look over your lifeline. Do you see any underlying themes that might arise? What made the highest points so emotionally satisfying? What have you learned from these events?

You now have a visual snapshot of your entire life. Choose one of these life events as the topic for your first legacy theme, "Forks in the Road." Keep the graph and list you generated and add to it as you remember new situations. Additional chapters for your life story may emerge from your list.

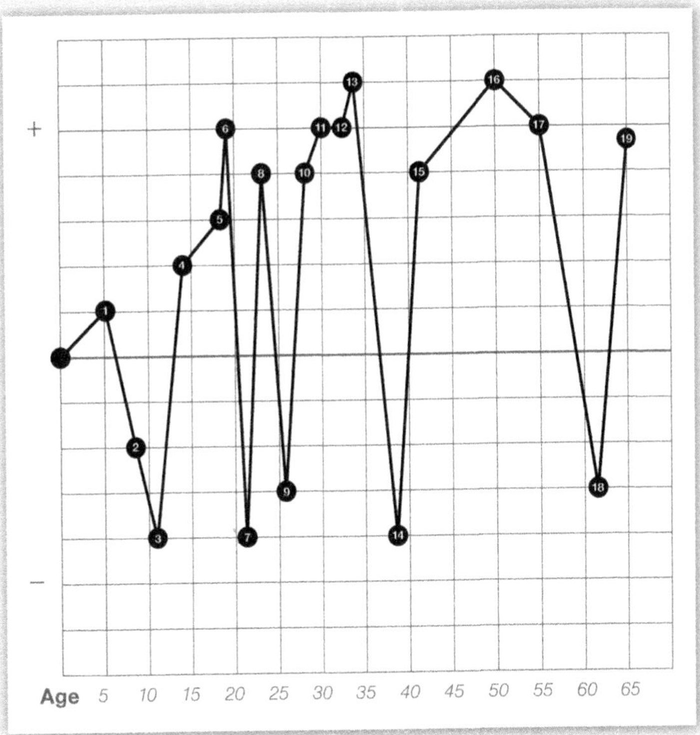

1. Started school
2. Moved to California
3. Dad killed
4. High school
5. Married
6. Baby
7. Mom died
8. College/baby
9. Divorce
10. USC grad school
11. Sweden
12. Baby
13. California
14. Brother killed
15. Baby
16. Ph.D.
17. Teaching
18. Lost home
19. New job opportunities

CHAPTER 14

Legacy Theme 2

My Family, My Self

"All happy families are alike; each unhappy family is unhappy in its own way." —LEO TOLSTOY

Most societies are built on the concept of family. *Family* refers to groups of people living together connected by birth, marriage, or choice. Families include parents, grandparents, aunts, uncles, and cousins and can wield powerful moral, emotional, social, and economic influence. Families by choice, such as close friends living together, and any other configuration, can exhibit equal force and bearing in a community.

Tolstoy's quote underlies the enduring dynamics of function and dysfunction: Some families work well, and others don't. What were the circumstances of your family of origin? How has its influence reached out across the generations?

Probing Questions

Take time to review the following questions. Each serves as a clarifying point that dips into your mind's recesses and helps you access long-forgotten memories. Some questions will resonate more than others.

Allow one or two of them to serve as the basis for your thematic story or lead you to other observations that can power the narrative. Keep in mind that they are just guidelines.

1. We all have a picture in our mind of the ideal family. What is yours? How did the family you were born into rate according to your *ideal*?
2. Thinking back to your childhood, what type of home environment did you grow up in? Did you feel safe and loved? Who made the decisions?
3. What were your family's expectations of you as a child and adolescent? Did this create tension in the household? How was it handled?
4. Thinking back on your family, what do you feel were your family's greatest strengths? What weaknesses may have caused problems?
5. We may feel more of an affinity for one family member vs. another. Who were you closest to, and why? Who were you most distant from, and why do you think so?
6. Does a particular family member stand out in your mind? Was this person eccentric, humorous, wildly successful, or the family black sheep? How did this person influence you?
7. What similarities and differences have you brought into your own family from your family of origin? Were there unexpected results? Do you recognize your parents in your own behavior today?
8. Did adoption play a role in your family of origin or adult family?
9. How are you like or unlike your mother? How are you like or unlike your father?
10. If you are unmarried and do not live with any blood relatives, how have you created a sense of "family" in your life?

Student Excerpt: My Family, My Self

When writing about family, our thoughts often go back to pleasant memories of beloved grandparents and other relatives. Here is one such story by Carol D'Agostino.

Each fall marked a ritual in my mother's family as I was growing up. To this day, the earthy aroma of decaying leaves triggers the memory of my grandma's kitchen, where strange and wonderful delicacies were created. A room that gave off a slight smell of gas from the pilot light on the stove as rich coffee bubbled in the old aluminum pot. A room where angel food cakes sat dripping with mint-chocolate icing running down onto a glass pedestal platter. A room where creamed potatoes, succulent rabbit or crisp, floured bullheads vanished from platters as quickly as she fried them up. A room where we stood in line at the stove with boiled potatoes cut open and streaming with melted butter while she ladled dairy-rich, creamy white codfish sauce ... along with the proverbial "Watch out for bones!" A room that held bowls of freshly picked black raspberries still hot from the garden sun. A room where fresh yellow snap beans were sautéed in butter and end-of-the-season cabbage wilted with vinegar that made your eyes water.

I can still see my grandma in her belted kitchen dress and laced, black shoes scurrying between the sink and the stove with a lace "hanky" tucked in her belt. I can see her lighting up filterless Camel cigarettes after her work was done and we all were happily fed. My roots ... my Dutch roots. It didn't matter that my father was German. I was Dutch through and through.

—Carol D'Agostino

Exercises: My Family, My Self

Buried deep within all of us are the sights, sounds, smells, and tastes of our childhood. The question is, how do we access those memories? When we do, we are often surprised with what comes up.

1. I REMEMBER: Set aside fifteen minutes, and make a list of everything you remember from when you were ten years old. Quickly jot down all the memories that come back to you. You don't need to write down full explanations, just triggers for you to use later. To get you started, here are some questions to consider: What books did you read? Did you like school? Who was your best friend? What games did you play? What was your favorite food? Where did you live? What trouble did you get into? What was your personality like?

You may be surprised how one memory leads to another when you let your mind roam freely. This list will give you insights that you may have forgotten from your life as a child and will motivate you to begin to write about family for Legacy Theme 2.

2. DRAW-A-ROOM: In this exercise you will access the right side of your brain—the more creative, intuitive side—as opposed to the left, logical, and analytical side. This is meant to be fun, free flowing, spontaneous. You will need a couple of large sheets of paper and crayons or marking pens. To begin, sit quietly and take a visual trip back to the childhood home you remember the best. Let your mind wander over the exterior, and then take a guided tour through the rooms in your home.

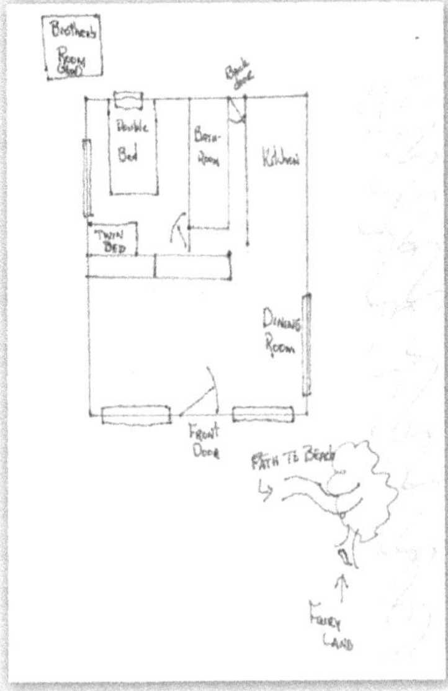

Drawing by Nedra Pautler.

First draw the outside, front view of the house. Remember, this is not a drawing lesson but an attempt to dig up forgotten memories associated with your childhood. Add all the features, i.e., roof, windows, doors, etc. Write the years you lived in the house below your drawing.

Second, draw the layout of the house as if you were looking down into it from above. Label the rooms, and show how they connected with one another. Third, choose one room in your house that held special meaning for you. It could be your bedroom, the living room, or the kitchen. Draw the layout of this room and include furniture, windows, closets, etc.

Now that you have drawn your home from different perspectives, many more memories will surface. Think back to the things that happened in this house or particular room. Who was there? What were the good memories? The bad ones?

You have now filled your memory bag with enough memories to begin writing on the second legacy theme, "My Family, My Self."

CHAPTER 15

Legacy Theme 3

The Meaning of Wealth

"When I was young I thought that money was the most important thing in life; now that I am old I know that it is." —OSCAR WILDE

The acquisition of money to buy goods and services is at the heart of our modern culture. This drive reaches across all societies and major institutions. Money permits access to education, health, housing, and private transportation. It offers respect and status. Yet it remains, for many, a limited resource. Without money, poverty becomes an epidemic of despair and hopelessness. Most of us learn our financial values early in life. We mimic those around us, picking up both good and bad habits. How we manage our wealth reflects how we see our world.

Probing Questions

Take time to review the following questions. Each serves as a clarifying point that dips into your mind's recesses and helps you access long-forgotten memories. Some questions will resonate more than others. Allow one or two of them to serve as the basis for your thematic story or lead you to other observations that can power the narrative. Keep in mind that they are just guidelines.

1. Most of us get our ideas about money from our family of origin. When you were growing up, how was money viewed in your family? Was there enough of it? Was your family considered working class, middle class, or wealthy?
2. Did your parents instill values about money when you were young? For instance, were you given an allowance? Were you required to get a job to earn your own spending money?
3. How did you learn about the meaning of wealth and money management? Was this learned at home, school, or later in life? Did you have a role model?
4. What was your first major purchase in life? How did you finance it?
5. You may have experienced fat or lean periods in your life concerning money. Have you ever gained a large amount of money over a short period of time? Have you ever lost a significant amount of money?
6. Have you borrowed money or loaned it out? What feelings accompanied these actions?
7. Over the years, have you moved from one level of society to another? What brought you there?
8. Do you spend money on the things you want in life, or do you prefer to save for the future?
9. What does money symbolize for you? Security? Safety? Power? Freedom?
10. What is the one important lesson you have learned about money?

Student Excerpt: The Meaning of Wealth

We all have unique ideas about money we have learned during our lifetime. Often our money values are learned from our parents, either from observation of their money habits or by being told the importance—or relative unimportance—of money. The following excerpt by Patty Tomaszewski recounts one lifelong money lesson learned from a parent.

Time is money. I don't know where I heard that, but the older I get, the truer I find it is.

When I was a little girl, and thought I would live forever, I learned "hustle" from my father, as well as the value of a dollar. He owned an excavation business and got paid based on jobs done. He worked seven days a week, as long as the daylight held. Sometimes it was longer. The crew he hired was, I'm sure, based on any number of factors, but the criteria I remember best was how fast they walked. If they came in to the garage looking for a job and moving briskly, they stood a good chance of being hired. Stroll in and you were going to stroll right back out, still unemployed. He could train them to operate equipment, but he couldn't train them about hustle. Both my parents reminded me often that if someone took $100 from you, you could always earn it back. If they kept you waiting twenty minutes, you could never get those minutes back. They were gone. The lesson: Be sure your time, as well as your money, is invested wisely. You cannot separate the two.

As I got older, I experienced the value of his lessons firsthand. I started my own real estate business and worked long hours, but nothing was more frustrating than customers or clients who kept me waiting. Except, perhaps, trying to figure out how to pay the bills. Two of his other lessons were: "Always pay your bills on time," and "Save at least 20 percent of your income." They were lessons cast in cement, and I was constantly relearning them. I started my real estate career in May of 1986—a single mother with a mortgage and two small boys. By the time I had my first closing that July, I had bills totaling $2,400 … and my commission check was $1,800. I had to rethink some of those rules and ignored them for a little while, which was uncomfortable. I tried to develop different rules that were easier to live with but had no success.

—Patty Tomaszewski

Exercise: The Meaning of Wealth

You may have reached a point in your writing where you feel stuck for new ideas. Or vice versa: So many ideas are flying toward you that you find it hard to focus and write. The clustering or mind-mapping technique helps you generate fresh ideas and focus for your stories. Tony Buzan and Gabriele Lusser Rico have written books on this topic if you wish to explore the concept in more detail. Here is how it works.

Think of clustering as a visual map of a brainstorming session. It is free association that results in a pictogram of words and ideas that build on one another. Your critical, analytical left brain is shut down for this exercise, and your free-flowing, intuitive right brain takes over. To begin, write the keyword or topic for your writing in the center of the paper. This word will trigger associations, and for the next three minutes you should quickly, and without censoring, write down all words that come to mind. Circle the word and connect it with a line to the word that prompted it. If a new, unconnected word arises, connect it directly to the keyword. Don't worry about getting all the connections correct; just keep your hand moving. When you are finished, you may see a pattern appear. Now you're ready to write.

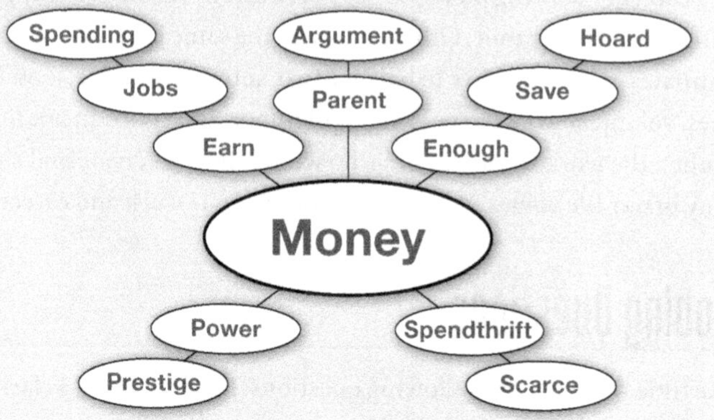

Adapted from *Writing the Natural Way* by Gabriele Lusser Rico.

CHAPTER 16

Legacy Theme 4

My Life's Work

> *"Choose a job you love, and you will never have to work a day in your life."* —CONFUCIUS

Most of us work to live; the lucky ones live to work. Those who are fortunate enough have discovered their passion and made it their life's work. Whether doctors, teachers, ironworkers, homemakers, or any one of a thousand other job titles, we spend a significant part of our lives building a career or earning money to support a family lifestyle. Many people change careers over time. Others stay with the same job for decades. Less fortunate people may have to balance two, sometimes three, jobs. Many times, volunteer work is a person's most important legacy. In one form or another, the work we do defines who we are. It helps create and sustain many of our life values. What is the story of your work and career life?

Probing Questions

Take time to review the following questions. Each serves as a clarifying point that dips into your mind's recesses and helps you access long-forgotten memories. Some questions will resonate more than others.

Allow one or two of them to serve as the basis for your thematic story or lead you to other observations that can power the narrative. Keep in mind that they are just guidelines.

1. When you were young, did you dream about what you wanted to be when you became an adult? Did you follow that dream? What became your life's work? How did you enter that field, and who influenced your decision?
2. Where a person lives may have a strong influence on the jobs and education available. Did your place of residence affect your career choice?
3. We devote time and energy to our work, but we also receive benefits other than monetary ones. What have been the greatest benefits from your chosen field of work? What have been the greatest challenges?
4. Many people hold a series of jobs over the course of their life. If you have worked at several jobs, which one did you find the most rewarding? Which one was the least rewarding?
5. Particularly in earlier decades, gender played a strong role in the careers open to women as compared to men. Did gender affect your choice of career? Were there positive and negative influences?
6. Did your life's work take you on one long, continuous journey, or did it involve a series of stops and starts? Did you like your work?
7. What primary motivators attracted you to your major life's work? Passion, power, money, service to community, proximity to home, less stress, responsibility?
8. How did your life's work make you a better person? What are you most proud of accomplishing through your work?
9. Did you have a mentor who helped you with your career? What recommendations would you give to someone interested in pursuing the work you perform?
10. If you could, would you do it all over again? What changes would you make?

Student Excerpt: My Life's Work

Work means different things to everyone. Some may feel that their life's work lies in their professional field, while others find it in the volunteer sector. Some, like Bonnie Bernell, feel that their entire life is their life's work.

I = work. I work. I work a lot. I value work. I have judgments about people who don't work. By that I mean those who are not productive. Productive, produce something. Do something. Learn something. Contribute something. People who hang out full time seem bad or wrong somehow. I know that part of my judgment is that I am not so good at hanging out, being still. I also know that stillness for me can be and has been good when I have let myself do it. I get clarity. I am creative from a place of stillness. I can feel good. I am not still very often, not often enough.

I have always worked, it seems. I worked in my father's medical office. I took typing and Gregg and Pitman shorthand at twelve or thirteen and worked when I was a high school student. I have had tons of jobs. I was a page at a Federal Reserve Bank. I sold Avon door to door, was a terrible secretary, and had an exhausting stint as a waitress in a fraternity for medical students at the University of Wisconsin (on a dare and a hope to meet guys). I couldn't figure out what I wanted to do. I dropped out of college multiple times—probably five, at least—because playing and drinking (which I haven't done in forty years) took over. I found psychology, or it found me. I was trying to work out my life. I had always loved art but knew, from the deepest place in my soul, that I had to be able to take care of myself financially and in every other way. No one else was going to be there for me, period.

I didn't ever think I was very smart, but I knew I worked hard. I had a catering business, wrote a book, taught graduate students, do therapy and all its aspects. Lots of jobs. I like to work. I like the feeling of having a place to go, a thing to do, a way to contribute, a means of helping people, at times. I always have projects, too. Lots of projects. I am best when I am immersed in some idea that I am exploring, creating, developing, marketing, and imagining, when I know that what I do makes the world a bit better because I did what I did.

—Bonnie Bernell

Exercise: My Life's Work

Your work life probably began when you were young. Perhaps your first job led you to your lifelong career. Or maybe it's a reminder of work you never want to do again. Some of your most significant milestones are connected to your work life.

Review the following memory joggers.

- What was the first job you ever had that involved a regular paycheck? How old were you?
- How did you get this job?
- What were your job responsibilities?
- What was the best part about this work? What did you not like about it?
- Did it lead to something bigger and better?
- Did it help you decide on what you did or did not want to do with your life?

Write a short paragraph about your "dream job." We've all been asked as children, "What do you want to be when you grow up?" Think back to your childhood dreams of your possible career. Was it an astronaut? Major league baseball player? Actor? What are your talents? What makes you happy? Let your imagination go, and freely fantasize about a job you would create for yourself.

Now you have jump-started your creative juices, and you are ready to write on your life's work.

CHAPTER 17

Legacy Theme 5

Self-Image and Well-Being

"The greatest of follies is to sacrifice health for any other kind of happiness." —ARTHUR SCHOPENHAUER

As Schopenhauer so wisely pointed out, good health is one of the primary components in our well-being. We often take our health for granted, until an illness or disease steps in and forces us to pay attention to what we eat, how we live, how we exercise and take care of our bodies. This may serve as a wake-up call to show us that there are many aspects of our health that we can control and improve.

Your health and body image may reflect one another. For instance, when people are in poor physical condition, their self-image typically takes a nosedive as well. It is hard to feel good about yourself when feeling unhealthy. Your life is likely marked by periods of both good and poor health. How has your health affected you over your lifetime? Did you "measure up" to the prevailing body ideal of the time when you were growing up? How did you cope with illness? Each of us is challenged in our own unique way.

Probing Questions

Take time to review the following questions. Each serves as a clarifying point that dips into your mind's recesses and helps you access long-forgotten memories. Some questions will resonate more than others. Allow one or two of them to serve as the basis for your thematic story or lead you to other observations that can power the narrative. Keep in mind that they are just guidelines.

1. When you think back over the course of your life, how do you assess your health? Has it been generally good, or have you been continuously challenged?
2. In each segment of your life—childhood, adolescence, adulthood—did your health status remain the same or did you experience changes due to unexpected illnesses or accidents? How has aging affected your health?
3. Throughout your life, what has been your body image? Did you see yourself as tall, short, weak, strong, thin, fat, attractive, or unattractive? Did you fit in with the prevailing norm? During adolescence, were you a late bloomer or did you develop early compared to your peers?
4. What does the mind-body connection mean to you? Does each have equal value? Do you treat their health aspects equally?
5. While life can be hard on us physically and mentally, we can also be hard on life—in other words, we don't always make the best choices for our well-being. How have you treated your body and mind over your lifetime?
6. If you have suffered serious injury or disease, how did it change you? Has your worldview changed in any way?
7. If you've suffered a mental health crisis, how did you handle it? Do you use preventative measures or medication? Has this affected your lifestyle?
8. How do you handle stress? Has too much stress been an issue in your life? What ways have you found to cope with it?

9. Have you ever been addicted to any substance? How did it begin, and where did it take you? How did you handle this issue?
10. If there was something you could change about your body, what would it be?

Student Excerpt: Self-Image and Well-Being

We all have the tendency to be overly critical of how we look, especially if we do not match the current fashion image. We may feel the need to diet, to dye our hair, or even to visit cosmetic surgeons. The following is how student Shawn Feisst appraised her body with a grateful eye.

> If I rewind my child's mind back to a time when I was really aware of any part of my body beyond fire-burning tonsils, it has to be my hair. Why didn't I get my mother's hair? She was born with black, black hair, which was very unusual for her English heritage. No, I got my father's English and Scottish hair, thin and fine. No girl's dream, I promise you. I have had to perm it, cut it, color it, all of the above.
>
> I think I could say that my arms and hands have provided the most for me in this life. They are strong and able. They have driven horses, lifted scuba tanks, built doll houses, carried paddle boards and canoes, written journals, held babies, supported headstands in yoga, and provided numerous hours of massage. The nail salon era was a quick affair, as I have grown to love my hands with their short nails and weathered skin. My hands are attached to a pair of very strong and sculpted arms, and they give me power many women and some men would love to have. Not sure I would trade them for hair.
>
> Author Anne Lamott said it best when describing *her* thighs. She calls them her old aunties. My thighs may not be sleek and long (thank God my daughter got those), but let me tell you how many hundreds of miles these thighs have taken this body up hills and over roads all across this country atop a bicycle or Nike shoes. They are soft now and more comfortable hidden beneath capris.

My familia has gifted me with good health and great longevity—my mother's family was cancer free and my father is a healthy eighty-five years old; his mother lived to one hundred and her mother to 103—and I am grateful, as I realize this is not the case for many.

—Shawn Feisst

Exercise: Self-Image and Well-Being

This exercise will provide you with a health overview. Use it as a reference to trigger your memories when you write about your health and well-being. On a separate sheet of paper, answer the following questions:

- What health problems or challenges did you endure as a child or adolescent? List both physical and emotional ones.
- What health problems or challenges have you endured as an adult? List both physical and emotional ones.
- How do you feel about your health today?

CHAPTER 18

Legacy Theme 6

The Male-Female Equation

"In politics, if you want anything said, ask a man. If you want anything done, ask a woman."

—MARGARET THATCHER

We are all born with a biological sex: male or female. Gender identity refers to how we feel about being a man or a woman, that is, our internal psychological and emotional sense of maleness or femaleness. This identity can vary with different periods of life. A young girl may grow up as a tomboy and strongly express her male attributes. A young boy may grow up delighting in the more feminine aspects of life and feel disinclined to participate in the rough-and-tumble world of sports and skinned knees. As sexual preference comes into play, further categorization may define us as lesbian, gay, bisexual, transgender (LGBT), or straight.

The male-female equation is one of the most powerful forces in life. As we mature and experience more of the world we live in, our gender identities either remain firm or become diffused. At some point we might begin questioning who we are and who we might want to become.

Probing Questions

Take time to review the following questions. Each serves as a clarifying point that dips into your mind's recesses and helps you access long-forgotten memories. Some questions will resonate more than others. Allow one or two of them to serve as the basis for your thematic story or lead you to other observations that can power the narrative. Keep in mind that they are just guidelines.

1. What was your first remembered experience of being male or female?
2. Did your family have strong expectations for how boys and girls should act? Were you given certain expectations to live up to that may have created problems? If you had a sibling of the opposite sex, was that person treated differently?
3. Childhood is often a time that is considered "genderless." During your childhood, were you ever confused about your gender identity?
4. When did you develop a first significant friendship with a person of the opposite sex? How was that different from a friendship you had with someone of the same sex?
5. Often in childhood we intuitively know something about "the birds and the bees," but when were you taught about sex and procreation? Who taught you? A family member, your peers, your school, or the media? Was the information accurate?
6. Were your initial male-female relationships positive experiences for you? How did they differ?
7. Were you ever sexually traumatized? How did this affect you immediately afterwards and later in life? Have you ever told anyone?
8. Did you ever wish you were of the opposite sex? How far did you take this thinking?
9. As an adult, what is your gender identity? All male, all female, or a mix of both? Is this a comfortable balance in your life?
10. Have your ideas about sexual roles and expectations changed over the course of your life? How do you feel about society's increasing tolerance to the expression of varied sexual orientations?

Student Excerpt: The Male-Female Equation

We first learn about intimate and sexual relationships and come in contact with the opposite gender during adolescence. This is when we define who we are. If our development fits with societal and cultural norms, the transition is often easy. However, many individuals also have stories of growing up too fast, as shown in the following excerpt by Marie Rowe.

> When I was twelve years old my breasts were quite well developed and I was definitely blooming into a curvy young woman. It was at this time that a stranger molested me. The "gas man" was a tall, imposing man with an Irish accent and a shock of thick black hair who came to our house to read the gas meter. He asked me if anyone was home, and I said: "No, just me." Big mistake! I innocently let him into the house and showed him where the meter was. After he'd finished jotting down the details, and just as I was ready to show him out, he suddenly plunged his hands inside my dress and started to fondle my breasts. He remarked that I had "nice titties." I lied that my father was sleeping upstairs and I was going to call him. The "gas man" smiled and winked at me as I showed him to the door.
>
> As soon as I saw him ride off on his bike, I ran to a kindly neighbor, Mrs. Nettleship, and told her what had happened. I was very upset, and she was so comforting. She gave me a big slice of chocolate cake and a large glass of milk. Her cake was the best I've ever tasted. Then she took me home, and we waited for my dad and grandfather to arrive from work. They were surprised to see her there, and she told them of the incident with the "gas man."
>
> My father turned to me and said, "Why would you want to tell a lie like that?"
>
> My grandfather agreed with him. "That's a terrible thing to say."
>
> "You'd better not tell your mother. You'll upset her with your lies," my father continued.
>
> I was devastated that they didn't believe me, while Mrs. Nettleship simply shook her head. She put her arm around me, kissed me on the cheek, and quietly said, "I'm sorry, love." Then she left.

From then on, I did everything I could to try and conceal my breasts—never wearing tight sweaters or clothing that revealed my shape. I also walked hunched over. My mother, who did not know of the incident with the "gas man," constantly told me to get my shoulders back and stick out my chest. It was many years before I could walk tall and feel proud to be a woman.

—Marie Rowe

Exercises: The Male-Female Equation

1. Look over the following questions as you begin to think about writing on gender. They will help clarify that gender is not a black-and-white concept.

- As a child, how did you see yourself in terms of gender? Were you all boy, all girl, a tomboy, or something else?
- How long did that perception last? What changed it?
- Who were your closest friends through your childhood? Through adolescence? Were your closest friends usually of the same gender as you?
- As an adult, what gender balance do you have concerning your closest friends?

2. Write a paragraph that describes you as a teenager. Write quickly, unsparingly, and with as much detail as you can recall. Write this in the third person as if you were describing yourself to someone who had never met you.

CHAPTER 19

Legacy Theme 7

The End of Life

"The fear of death follows from the fear of life. A man who lives fully is prepared to die at any time."

—MARK TWAIN

To live is to be courageous. As Mark Twain reminds us, to live a full life we must accept that we, too, will one day die. You may have experienced the death of someone close to you early in life, thus pushing death into the forefront of your "reality" from an early age. Or you may have had a close call with death and been given a second chance to appreciate what you almost lost. These profound experiences shape the perception of death: You might fear dying, or perhaps you've accepted it as inevitable.

All cultures have rituals and ceremonies that mark the end of life. How were death and dying dealt with when you were growing up? For many, the end of life may be seen as the beginning of something else. What are your views about death and dying?

Probing Questions

Take time to review the following questions. Each serves as a clarifying point that dips into your mind's recesses and helps you access long-forgotten memories. Some questions will resonate more than others. Allow one or two of them to serve as the basis for your thematic story or lead you to other observations that can power the narrative. Keep in mind that they are just guidelines.

1. Your first experiences with death often lay the groundwork for your acceptance of or fear of death. What was your first experience with death? Did it involve a person or pet? How did you react? How was it explained to you?
2. Was death and dying a topic that you were able to talk about in your family circle? How did those around you view death? Did you accept these explanations? Did they instill fear or comfort in you?
3. Funerals and memorials are part of our cultural rituals to bring closure to a death. What was the first funeral you attended? Have you ever viewed a corpse? Describe a funeral you attended.
4. There are times, especially with suicide, when the death of someone close brings up feelings of guilt. Did you ever feel you were responsible for another's death? How did this impact your life?
5. Did you ever experience a close call with your own death? Did this change your thinking or your life values?
6. Whose death in particular has affected you the most? How did you react? Did you feel helpless, guilty, angry? Has it, or can it, ever be resolved?
7. Have you ever helped a family member or friend through the dying process? Was it a positive or negative experience? Did it change you in any way?
8. Suicide may be the most difficult death to understand and accept. Have you ever considered suicide? Were you close to anyone who committed suicide? How did you feel?
9. What do you think happens to your body, mind, and soul upon death?
10. Have you ever thought about your own death? How do you want to die? Who do you want to be with you?

Student Excerpt: The End of Life

The first encounter with death is a unique voyage. Some remember being forced to look into a coffin; others remember when their beloved dog died or maybe a classmate fell ill and died. Whatever experience you have had with death, it has left its imprint on you. This story by Pam Hueckel explains that not all deaths are equal.

> Without a doubt, my father's death affected me the most profoundly of all. He was nearly ninety-four, but I was not prepared. I felt as if my entire life had been swept out from under me, for I'd lost not only my father but also my work as his sole caregiver, and my home. For the first year, I struggled with disorientation, fear about the future, and intense feelings of guilt. I could not stop replaying in my mind the events of his last months—his final week in particular—the confusion, my misunderstandings, endless decisions, weeks in and out of the hospital, discussions and arguments with doctors, and his attempts to use every last ounce of his waning strength to communicate his needs, while placing his entire trust in me. I knew guilt was common following a death and that at some point I would need to forgive myself and let it go. But I couldn't. Others tried to help: "Put it into perspective ..." one friend urged. "You're being *way* too hard on yourself," advised another. Maybe so, but I wanted Dad back long enough to tell him how deeply sorry I was.
>
> On the eve of the first anniversary of Dad's death, I spent the night in an unusual state of wakeful sleep. I didn't toss and turn, overcome by painful memories and tears, as I'd so often done during the previous months. Nor was I fully asleep, or dreaming, but somewhere between wakefulness and sleep. I felt relaxed and let my thoughts carry me, as I sometimes do at night, because in the stillness they often lead to an insight about me or my life with others.
>
> In the very early morning, an image arose, quite unexpectedly, in full view of my mind's eye. My father was wearing his favorite royal-blue jacket and his characteristic, buoyant smile. Behind his right shoulder sat my mother, quietly looking on, also smiling. "God speaks to us in pictures. ..." The doubts of the previous year

vanished as the knowing welled up from deep within me. Mom and Dad were both okay; in fact, they looked pleased as punch. Whatever mistakes I'd made and suffering I'd caused were in the past. After a flood of grateful tears had dried, I fell asleep, finally convinced that all was well.

—Pam Hueckel

Exercises: The End of Life

Writing about death in your life story may be particularly difficult. Death is a natural part of life, but most of us live in a death-denying bubble. We find it difficult to contemplate our own death and fear for the death of loved ones. Put aside your fears for a few minutes, and answer the following questions. Often, facing our greatest fear gives us strength and insight in unexpected ways. This will open your thinking about death as you prepare to write.

1. Imagine that you will die within one year, and answer the following prompts on a separate sheet of paper.

- The first person I would tell is ...
- There are several things I would do during the one year. They include ...

Have you considered doing any of these things even if you are in good health now?

From this list, compose a short, half-page story on what you would do if you had but one year to live.

2. Epitaphs can be funny or serious, but their purpose is to condense one's life into a short, succinct sentence. Write your own epitaph. What would you say about your life within this brief space?

CHAPTER 20

Legacy Theme 8

From Secular to Spiritual

"Science without religion is lame. Religion without science is blind." —ALBERT EINSTEIN

Spirituality is not synonymous with religion but rather embraces all religions. It is the yearning to understand what we all feel when we stand on the brink of the unknown abyss and try to make sense of it all. Spirituality exists in our searching for what lies beyond and in looking for meaning and purpose. Where did we come from? Why are we here? Where are we going? Our lives are tossed back and forth, from knowing to unknowing, and we still keep living to the best of our abilities.

How you derive your strength for the road ahead is a deeply personal choice. Formal religion finds support in Christian, Judaic, Hindu, and Islamic tenets, among many others. Nature comforts the soul with its pastoral hills, meandering streams, vast oceans, and towering mountains. From secular to spiritual, each of us finds our own source of comfort and meaning.

Probing Questions

Take time to review the following questions. Each serves as a clarifying point that dips into your mind's recesses and helps you access long-forgotten memories. Some questions will resonate more than others. Allow one or two of them to serve as the basis for your thematic story or lead you to other observations that can power the narrative. Keep in mind that they are just guidelines.

1. Your first experience with religion and spiritual beliefs usually comes from your family. As a child, did you attend formal religious services regularly? Did both of your parents participate in the church? Did you ever question your beliefs during this time?
2. Adolescence is a time of questioning, rebellion, and searching for answers. During your teenage years, how did you view your spiritual beliefs? Were they changing in any way?
3. Was there a time in your adult life when you fell away from your religious or spiritual beliefs? What happened, and was there resolution?
4. Have you ever had a significant spiritual experience? What happened? Did this reaffirm or change your original beliefs?
5. Significant people in our lives often open doors for our continuing spiritual development. In your lifetime, have you had spiritual role models, either living or dead, who may have changed your beliefs and helped you grow? How were they important to you?
6. Books written by great spiritual teachers help us grow in our beliefs. Was there a specific book, philosophy, or song that has changed you in any way?
7. When we come into contact with new cultural and religious beliefs, our own may be questioned and challenged. What has been your experience with this?
8. Have you ever been pressured to change your spiritual beliefs? Have you ever tried to convert someone to your belief system? What were the outcomes and ramifications?

9. What part of your spiritual journey are you on at this point in time? What challenges lie ahead for you?
10. What is a core belief that you hold about yourself and your place in the world? How is it reflected in your life?

Student Excerpt: From Secular to Spiritual

Whether we connect spirituality to religion or not, spirituality does have to do with the nontangible, ethereal aspects of life. We all struggle to make sense of our world, especially when something inexplicable happens. In this story, Dawn Vanderloo shows how an ordinary drive became a spiritual experience.

> Something spiritual happens to me on the open road. More than in any church, more than when bare-footing on a beach or cresting a mountain path, more than in a morning prayer … the road is the place where I most often touch God.
>
> I'm not sure when these spiritual experiences began. What I do specifically remember is a drive from Salt Lake City back to my former home in Palo Alto in 1993. For a woman who was usually euphoric behind the wheel, this one stretch of road was hell on Earth. Heading west out of Salt Lake City on Interstate 80, I had to cover more than 500 miles of wasteland before hitting Reno and ascending into the beauty of the High Sierras. This area was comprised of short hill ranges and their subsequent valleys, all colored brown. Dull brown. Stale brown. Pig-shit brown. It was the most boring drive, and I dreaded it every time.
>
> I was in a calm, contemplative state and decided to spend a few quiet minutes in prayer. And it was in that place of contemplation that I crossed the threshold into my cathedral. Call it an altered state. Call it heightened consciousness. Call it the love of God. All I know is that it was transcendental. I was enveloped in unconditional love; my sense of universal connection was expansive. And as I looked out over the once-brown wasteland through which I

drove, all I could see were the colorful auras of all that existed there ... blurry spectrums of color everywhere.

Wow... so this was rapture.

And then I was joined by an angel, who I couldn't see but knew was there. He sat in my back seat—a little too large for the rear of my SAAB convertible—but he didn't complain as he stretched his long arms out across the back and smiled as the wind hit his face. In fact, he was thrilled with my speed. I found myself driving 100 ... 110 miles per hour, literally passing cars and a couple of parked patrolmen as if I were a silver bullet with a cloak of invisibility surrounding me. And this state of mystical rapture lasted for miles ... for hours ... until I hit Reno, where my celestial guest left and the laws and confines of earth restricted me again.

—Dawn Vanderloo

Exercise: From Secular to Spiritual

Spirituality and religion both grapple with the bigger questions in life: What is the meaning of life? How did I get here? What happens when we die? Religion is organized around a set of beliefs and rituals that help followers answer such questions. Spirituality focuses on the nonphysical, more intuitive aspects of life in order to understand its meaning. Both lead to transcending the self. The following exercise, creating a spiritual map, will sidestep your analytical left brain and allow you to freely explore your spiritual history. Allow yourself thirty minutes to chart the peaks and valleys of your life.

You will need a large sheet of unlined paper, as well as pens, crayons, or markers. Set aside a time when you can quietly reflect on your life without being disturbed. To create your spiritual map, briefly answer the following questions:

- What are your spiritual beliefs?
- How did you come to believe them?
- Have your beliefs changed over the years?

Jot down a list of the peaks and valleys of your life from childhood to the present. Include your successes as well as your failures, times of regret, fear, dismay, joy, and so on. Recall what you were feeling during each situation. Create a symbol or word that describes each event.

On your sheet of paper, draw a shape that represents your life. This will be the shape or space that contains the peaks and valleys of your life.

Using your markers or crayons, draw the highs and lows of your life on your map. Use the symbols and words, or draw pictures to identify your life's spiritual journey.

Have fun with this. You do not need to share your map with anyone else. This will open your perspective to new ways of thinking about the spiritual highs and lows in life.

This map will provide a visual representation of your life's most significant moments. You may see connections that you had not considered previously. For the first time you may be aware of the emotional aspects of each of the experiences. You will see how far you have come in your spiritual life and may find new directions for where you are going.

Refer to your map as you write your Secular to Spiritual story.

CHAPTER 21

Legacy Theme 9

My Life Goals

"You are never too old to set another goal or to dream a new dream." —C.S. LEWIS

As a child, what were some of your hopes and dreams? You may have followed through on these old dreams, or perhaps you moved in an entirely different direction in life once you reached adulthood. At times you simply followed along the course life took you, while on other occasions you planned, prepared, and worked toward your goal. Goals are for achieving and must be personal to be effective. It must be *your* goal and not one someone else has set for you.

Each of us lives within a defined life process, one that we create ourselves. Sometimes we choose short-term goals, while at other times we set lifelong challenges that we may not always achieve. Lessons are learned, and we move on. When you set goals for your future, you express faith in yourself. You trust in your ability to succeed. What is your history of dreams and goals?

Probing Questions

Take time to review the following questions. Each serves as a clarifying point that dips into your mind's recesses and helps you access long-forgotten memories. Some questions will resonate more than others. Allow one or two of them to serve as the basis for your thematic story or lead you to other observations that can power the narrative. Keep in mind that they are just guidelines.

1. As a child, did you dream about a career or interest you would later pursue in life? Or did that passion come at another time?
2. Who inspired you towards a particular life goal? Was it someone you knew, a parent or teacher? Did it come through reading about someone you respected, or did you learn on your own?
3. At times you may be your biggest supporter, and at other times your own worst enemy. Which of your personal characteristics helped you achieve your life goals: intelligence, creativity, physical appearance, spiritual values, perseverance? Which ones tended to work against you? How did you handle those situations?
4. What do you feel are your most important life achievements? How did they challenge you? What help did you receive along the way?
5. Was there a time in your life when you had no discernible goals or dreams? What was that like? What enabled you to refocus on achieving your goals?
6. Did you ever fail to achieve an important goal? How did you react? What did you learn about yourself when you lost?
7. Do you usually have a strong emotional investment in your life goals? Are they strongly tied to your identity?
8. Have you worked closely with someone else to help him or her achieve a particular goal? Was it a positive or negative experience?
9. Is there still one major goal you continue to strive towards? Has this been a lifelong goal?

10. As C.S. Lewis said, we are never too old for goals. Are there goals you still hope to achieve? What are your dreams today? What are you doing to reach them?

Student Excerpt: My Life Goals

You may think you are not a goal setter, but everyone keeps a list, mental or written, of things they plan to do or hope to accomplish. While some people love to make lists and cross things off as they are completed, others simply wing it through life. The following excerpt by Robert McKechnie shows that no matter how old you are, there's always room for aspirations.

I'm seventy-one years old. Most people of this age think it's time to plunk down into the La-Z-Boy, flip the feet up, and relax. If I had any sense, I'd join them. Be assured—I don't have any sense. I have aspirations.

My old-age aspirations started several years ago. I started writing grant proposals to benefit the tiny high school where I served as the only guidance counselor. I succeeded in bringing in funds to purchase musical instruments. Now grant writing is in my blood. If things work out, I'll be able to go anyplace in the world while working at the same time.

I want to enrich the home Kris and I share, making sure everything works and the household remains quiet, comfortable, and happy. At the same time, I would like to carve out more time for travel. I'm planning a month-long trip to Madrid next September.

My vision for the future also calls for enriching the lives of my son, his wife, and their twin daughters. I have two things in mind, a cruise from Barcelona to Athens and a trip to Disney World in Florida. I would love to spice it up a bit for them, helping them become a little worldlier and adding to their education in a way that is great fun for everyone. Financially this is out of reach now, but I envision a deeper prosperity in the future. Anything's possible.

Yes, I have aspirations. When we moved to Palm Springs in 1997, I created "The I'm Not Dead Yet" program for myself. If the universe has given me life, I better use it. In fact, I would go so far as to say that if I'm given life but don't use it to serve others and enjoy myself, I would be committing a sin. Death will come soon enough—too soon, actually. I'm ready to embrace life as never before. And I am grateful.

—Robert McKechnie

Exercises: My Life Goals

1. GOALS AND ACCOMPLISHMENTS: This exercise will help you focus on the importance of goal setting throughout your life. Some people were raised in a goal-setting environment, while others learned to achieve goals in different ways. Answer the following questions:

- Was your family goal oriented? How did this affect you?
- What was the first major personal goal you remember accomplishing?
- Over time, how have your life goals changed? What were some of your important ones …
    - as a child?
    - as a teenager?
    - as a young adult?
    - in middle age?
    - today?

2. BUCKET LIST: Not everyone sets goals, but most still have things they wish to see or do before they die. Consider these unfulfilled desires your "bucket list" or "wish list." On a separate sheet of paper, write down all the things you still wish to do in your lifetime. It may be to take a trip to the Great Wall of China or to hold your first grandchild. The important point is to simply write it down quickly without censoring your thoughts and ideas. Let your thoughts flow onto the paper no matter how impossible they may seem.

After you have written twenty to thirty items on your list, it is time to refine it and cross off the ones you are least likely to achieve. For instance, if you are in your seventies and have on your list to play quarterback for the UCLA Bruins, you should probably let that one go. Next choose one of the simpler items on your list and get started. Maybe you have written that you want to run a 5K. The first step would be to buy the running shoes and begin walking around your neighborhood. This will motivate you to continue to accomplish the items on your bucket list. Remember that the list is a work in progress and can change over time. New ideas will come to you, and some of the earlier ones will lose their attractiveness; if they do, cross them off the list. The point of the bucket list is to complete the tasks you have listed and attain self-fulfillment.

CHAPTER 22

Legacy Theme 10

My Legacy Letter

"Carve your name on hearts, not tombstones. A legacy is etched into the minds of others and the stories they share about you." —SHANNON L. ALDER

Each life is significant, and we all want to be remembered for something. One way for you to do this is to write down your values, your hopes, and the life lessons you hope to impart to your family and others you care about. In doing so, you will be looking into your past and reviewing the gifts and lessons you learned from your ancestors as well as those you gleaned from your own life. A legacy letter is your chance to express your gratitude, to offer nonlegally binding instructions, and to hand down some life observations, personal values, and lessons learned. In this way, you will discover what you value the most and pass this on to future generations. The process provides you with deep personal satisfaction and recognition of the value of your life.

Probing Questions

Take time to review the following questions. Each serves as a clarifying point that dips into your mind's recesses and helps you access long-forgotten memories. Some questions will resonate more than others. Allow one or two of them to serve as the basis for your thematic story or lead you to other observations that can power the narrative. Keep in mind that they are just guidelines.

1. Who will be the recipients of your legacy letter? Family? Friends? Future generations? Picture a great-great-grandchild you will never know. What do you want him or her to know about you and your life?
2. What will be the central theme of your legacy? Expressions of love? Your life values? Your spiritual values? Lessons learned? Wishes for the future? All of these?
3. We are all governed and guided by our life values and philosophy. What values have you lived by? How did you acquire those values and beliefs? Did they come from your parents, teachers, or community?
4. Each generation is formed by the culture and period of time when they lived. What wisdom will your generation leave behind as a legacy?
5. What concerns do you have for the next generation? What advice can you give them?
6. Our passions and sustaining joys are what make life tolerable even in the darkest of times. What gives you great joy in this life?
7. What accomplishments are you most proud of that you wish to share with others?
8. Some of our most valuable lessons come from our mistakes. What mistakes have you made and what lessons did you learn?
9. What strengths and values do you wish to pass on to your children?
10. When would you like your Legacy Letter to be read? On what occasion?

Student Excerpt: My Legacy Letter

Being remembered is a universal human need. One way you can do this is to write a letter to your children and grandchildren, specifying your beliefs, values, and hopes for the future. Vickie Stam has written one such letter, meant to be read at her funeral.

Dear family and friends,
I would like you to travel with me for a moment along the roads that marked my journey. My voyage left me with several profound thoughts. Many of you witnessed my trials and triumphs throughout the years.

I felt blessed. Still, something was missing in my life. My divorce left a black cloud hanging over me. I felt lost as I grieved for the one thing that could restore my heart. I wanted my son in my life where I knew he belonged. The young man that I gave birth to and raised was within my reach and yet so far away. Jarod paid a high price for his parents' divorce.

I hope that anyone sitting here today will realize how wrong it is to inflict such horrendous pain on another human being when they could simply choose not to. If you are hearing this letter than you must know that I have finally been relieved of that pain. My advice to anyone who is divorced is that you never use your children to hurt one another. I would advise you to choose a road that is destined for healing.

Now that you are a father, Mason, I hope that you love your child unconditionally. There was nothing more that I wanted in life than to be a mother. I am grateful for the wonderful memories of raising my children. I am proud of you, Mason, for your integrity to work and provide for your family. You once said to me, "Money can't buy happiness, but neither does poverty, so I am content to live somewhere in the middle."

I thank God for bringing my husband, John, into my life. In the midst of all the chaos in our lives we found each other. John blessed me with his faith and strong values, and I loved him deeply. I want to quote a friend of mine who once said to me, "He must be a breath of fresh air for you," when she spoke of John. I can't imagine my life without him.

I am happy that God chose all of you to touch my life. It's alright to remember me with laughter and with tears.

Last but not least, I hope you will celebrate my life by sharing my favorite dessert. For those of you who know me well, know that rich chocolate cake with thick chocolate frosting is simply too good to pass up.

—Vickie Stam

Exercises: My Legacy Letter

1. PONDERING YOUR LEGACY: When you write your legacy letter, you are expressing the values and life lessons you wish to pass on to your progeny. You are not writing a will and leaving your valuables or possessions but rather the intangibles of who you are and the lessons you have learned. This is a priceless gift for posterity. Consider the following questions as you prepare to write your legacy letter.

- Leaving your legacy to another is an act of love. Who would be the recipients of such a letter?
- If you could have received a legacy letter from someone, who might that be and what would you have liked to know?
- What is a difficult experience that you might mention in your letter, and how would you explain it?
- If your loved ones could remember only two facts about the life you lived, what would they be?

2. DRAWING YOUR LEGACY TREE: Imagine your life as a tree and you as its trunk. The roots represent your ancestors, and the branches and leaves your descendants. On a sheet of paper, draw a large tree with roots and branches on it. Next, list the gifts, talents, and challenges you have received from your ancestors on the root system of your tree. On the trunk, list the strengths and qualities that make up your personality. Finally, on the branches and leaves, list all the talents, values, and gifts you are passing on to your descendants. Enjoy the freedom of creative expression as you draw and color your tree to replicate your life. You will have a visual image of both your past and your future.

You can use this illustration to enhance your legacy letter writing.

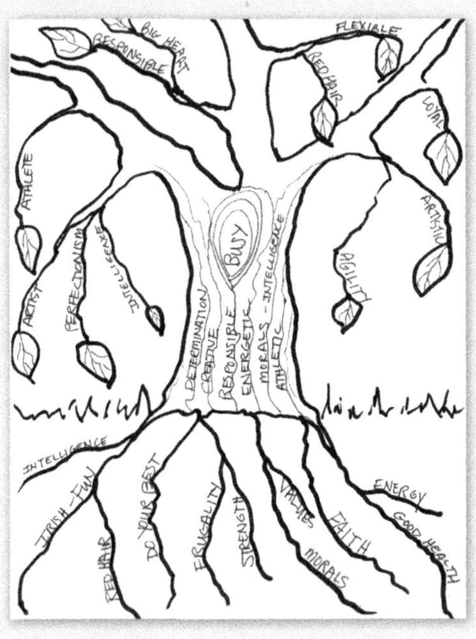
BIG HEART
RESPONSIBLE
FLEXIBLE
RED HAIR
LOYAL
ATHLETE
ARTISTIC
PERFECTIONISM
INTELLIGENCE
BUSY
INTELLIGENCE
AGILITY
ARTIST
DETERMINATION
CREATIVE
RESPONSIBLE
ENERGETIC
MORALS - INTELLIGENCE
ATHLETIC
INTELLIGENCE
IRISH - FUN
RED HAIR
DO YOUR BEST
FRUGALITY
STRENGTH
VALUES
FAITH
MORALS
ENERGY
GOOD HEALTH

CHAPTER 23

Adding Rooms

25 Additional Legacy Themes

When you have written your stories based on the ten core legacy themes, you will have produced an original life story of about 7,000–8,000 words. However, you may have more stories to tell. What you have written so far will give you a solid foundation for your life story. But just as each life story is never really complete, you can always add color, context, and flavor to yours.

We live in a bountiful world of opportunity. We sample new experiences as we move through the time frames of our lives. You may have filled your moments with an extravaganza of doing: You have traveled and celebrated your cultural heritage, you are passionate about your hobbies, you have shown courage in action, you have served your country, and you have loved others. Below you will find a list of twenty-five separate legacy themes. Read through them to see if any resonate with you.

- Legacy Theme 11: Life Values
- Legacy Theme 12: My Passions
- Legacy Theme 13: Art and Beauty
- Legacy Theme 14: Food and Drink
- Legacy Theme 15: Music in My Life
- Legacy Theme 16: My Literary Life
- Legacy Theme 17: Greatest Achievements

- Legacy Theme 18: Courage
- Legacy Theme 19: Cultural Heritage
- Legacy Theme 20: Creativity
- Legacy Theme 21: Friendships
- Legacy Theme 22: Travels
- Legacy Theme 23: My Pets
- Legacy Theme 24: Risks in My Life
- Legacy Theme 25: Sporting Life
- Legacy Theme 26: Natural Disasters and Accidents
- Legacy Theme 27: Life After Retirement
- Legacy Theme 28: The Art of Forgiveness
- Legacy Theme 29: Life Miracles
- Legacy Theme 30: Embarrassing Moments
- Legacy Theme 31: Siblings
- Legacy Theme 32: The Historical Times of My Life
- Legacy Theme 33: The First Time
- Legacy Theme 34: Children and Grandchildren
- Legacy Theme 35: Crime and Punishment

The twenty-five additional legacy themes are designed to capture your common and not-so-common life experiences. All reflect nuanced lives. Read over a few of the themes in this chapter and see which ones interest you and mirror your life experiences. Be sure to examine ones you might not initially be interested in—some of your best stories might be nestled within the following themes. Finally, read the questions and begin writing your own two- to three-page stories. Understanding how all of these pieces will fit together comes later. For now just keep on writing.

Legacy Theme 11: Life Values

"Your beliefs become your thoughts,
Your thoughts become your words,
Your words become your actions,
Your actions become your habits,
Your habits become your values,
Your values become your destiny."

—MAHATMA GANDHI

Your personal values help you live your life to the fullest expression. You obtain your values from your parents and upbringing, education, culture, and life experiences. These factors determine what you believe, how you act, and the decisions you make during the course of your life. They include your notions and opinions about family, love, divorce, religion, government, integrity, education, service to others, and self-control.

Values are usually constant, but they can and do change over time. They serve as guideposts, stakes in the ground, and lines in the sand, framing the world you believe in and are a part of. When your values are in sync with your decisions and the life you lead, life is good. When you are out of alignment with your values, you feel stressed and unhappy. Knowing your values will help you live a full and meaningful life.

1. It may be difficult to know exactly what your values are. Think back over your life, and remember a time when you were the proudest of an accomplishment. What happened? What value was expressed in that moment of pride?
2. What are your most important life values? Did you embrace them early in life or later? Did they derive from family influence, church, or community?
3. Which personal life values have changed over time for you? What were the circumstances that led to a change?

4. Which of your life values do you take the most pride in? If you were to prioritize your values, which one would be first? Why?
5. Do you have life values that are difficult for you to live up to? Why is that? Are they unchangeable?
6. We have all failed, at one time or another, to live up to our values. Which particular failure has caused you the greatest sadness? What were the ramifications?
7. Controversial life values surround abortion, the death penalty, homosexuality, and the legalization of drugs. What are your thoughts on these issues?
8. When your values are in alignment with your life, you feel good. Has there ever been a time when this was not the case? A time when your values did not fit with the life you were leading? What happened? Did you change your actions or your values?
9. The cultures and societies we live in exert a strong force on our personal values. Do you think an erosion of life values has occurred over the past few decades? If so, how were values better in the past?
10. Make a list of your top ten values. When you look over the list, are you still living up to those values? If you could fulfill only one of those values, which one would it be and why?

Legacy Theme 12: My Passions

"If you don't know what your passion is, realize that one reason for your existence on earth is to find it."

—OPRAH WINFREY

Your passions fuel your best work, give sustenance to your desires, and express your true self. When you are passionate, you are in tune with who you really are; your talents, your possibilities, and your self-confidence increase. Your energy soars when you are passionate. When your passions are in alignment with your authentic self, there are no limits. To live a passion-filled life, you must first know what your passions are. What dreams do you have that you may never have had the opportunity to realize? What excites you and gets you out of bed in the morning? Passion resides in all of us.

1. What were your major talents and abilities as a child? What were you excited about doing? Were these talents hobby related, sports related, school based?
2. Most of us have natural-born interests or talents. What were yours? What were you naturally good at doing? What did you enjoy doing so much that time seemed to stop when you were engaged in it?
3. Did your talents fit with the plans your family had for you? Or did you have your own ideas about what was best? Did you nurture your talents? Have they served you well in life?
4. Did your passions change as you moved into adolescence? What became your primary interests? Did you follow your dream?
5. As an adult, have your passions changed or evolved? How? Was there a situation such as injury that forced you to give up a passion? How did that affect you?
6. Are your passions primarily pursued by and for yourself? How are others involved?
7. Have your passions taken you down unexpected roads? What opportunities did they lead to?
8. What really excites you today? What are your major passions in this stage of your life?
9. How have your passions served you over your lifetime? How have they challenged you? What victories did you achieve? Was it all worth it?
10. If you could develop a new passion in life, what would that be? What is holding you back?

Legacy Theme 13: Art and Beauty

"Art attracts us only by what it reveals of our most secret self." —JEAN-LUC GODARD

You need not consider yourself an artist to appreciate the arts and the beauty that surrounds you. To be artful is to both create and appreciate beauty. When you witness something beautiful, it fills you with a sense of joy and happiness. We all respond differently to works of art, and thus there is no all-encompassing definition of beauty. What you regard as beautiful may have no meaning whatsoever to someone else. What do you regard as beautiful? How have you nurtured your love of art over the years?

1. What was the first time you remember being struck by the beauty of something? Was it a work of art? Something in nature?
2. In your childhood home, did your parents have paintings on the walls? Did this inspire an interest in art? Who influenced you?
3. Most education includes an art appreciation class. Do you have a formal education in art, or is it something that you have learned on your own?
4. What genre of art do you prefer? Abstract? Modern? Classical? Realist? Do you collect original pieces of art? How did you acquire them?
5. Are you an artist? Have you taken painting or sculpture lessons? If so, have you had any public exhibits?
6. As an artist or connoisseur, what is your favorite artistic style? Has that changed over the years?
7. Our travels may bring us in contact with major museums and galleries around the world. Have you visited any major galleries? What are your most memorable experiences?
8. The *Mona Lisa* is now housed behind glass in the Louvre because so many people have traveled to view it. If you could view one piece of artwork in person, what would it be?
9. Do you have a favorite artist? What about this artist appeals to you?

10. Art is a form of communication between the artist and the viewer. Have you ever been so inspired by a work of art that you changed your ideas or feelings about something? How were you changed?

Legacy Theme 14: Food and Drink

"One cannot think well, love well, sleep well, if one has not dined well." —VIRGINIA WOOLF

Does the thought of steak, a baked potato smothered in butter and sour cream, and rich desserts leave you salivating for more, while the thought of tofu, spinach, and brussels sprouts turns your stomach? Do you enjoy wine with your meal? Your likes and dislikes of certain foods are often rooted in your past. Was there a particular food that you hated as a child yet were forced to eat? Were you reminded to "clean your plate" because of all the starving children in the world? This theme offers you the chance to explore what you like to eat and cook, your eating habits and preferences, and the role food and drink play in your life.

1. Has food or drink affected your state of health in some form? How and what did you do? Did you ever change your eating habits to become healthier?
2. What is the role of restaurants and dining in your life? Do you eat out often? Think of an early memory dining out in a restaurant. Did your family have a favorite restaurant?
3. Do you live to eat rather than eat to live? Discuss the impact of your philosophy on your health and well-being. What about alcohol? Do you enjoy a glass of wine with dinner?
4. Is there a food you love that you cannot eat? Perhaps you are allergic to it or for health reasons are not allowed to eat it. How does that make you feel? Share your frustrations and anger over not being free to eat your favorite food.

5. Do you have family recipes that you still use? Are you a keeper of family culinary traditions? Are you a collector of recipes? Write one of your favorite recipes into your story.
6. Are you a "creative" cook? Or do you follow recipes precisely? Did you ever have to improvise a meal on the spur of the moment for an unexpected guest? Write about it.
7. Is there a food or wine that you love and can never get enough of? Discuss cravings. Have you ever had a craving for a certain food?
8. Cakes, cookies, ice cream, pies, all the sweet things in life. Are you a slave to your sweet tooth? What sweets rule your life? Describe a memorable moment related to food.
9. Was food used as a reward or punishment as a child? How did your family view food? Was it standard, everyday fare? Or did your parents experiment and try new things?
10. Were you raised on meat and potatoes? Did your parents make you sit at the table until you cleaned your plate?

Legacy Theme 15: Music in My Life

"Music expresses that which cannot be said and on which it is impossible to be silent." —VICTOR HUGO

Music is a means of expressing emotions, feelings, and experiences through the medium of sound. You do not need to be a great musician in order to appreciate, value, and be transported by music. When you listen to Stravinsky's *The Rite of Spring*, you can feel spring bursting forth with energetic vigor. Listening to your country's national anthem brings up feelings of patriotism and love for your nation. There are various genres of music to fit different moods: classical, rock, pop, country, electronic, folk, gospel, hip-hop, jazz, reggae, rhythm and blues, soul, and more.

Music has always been a part of what it means to be human. Archaeologists have discovered flutes carved from bone dating back to prehistoric times. Music is such an important component of our lives that we may tend to take it for granted and underestimate the significance it plays. Music can inspire and fuel your creativity. What has been the role of music in your life? Are you a musician or an appreciator of music? Or both?

1. What is the first song you remember from childhood? Was it sung to you, or did you hear it on the radio? Did you sing in a church choir? Any choir? What was that like for you?
2. What became your first favorite style of music? How old were you, and how long did this stage last? Did it become a lifelong passion?
3. Who is your all-time favorite musical performer?
4. When you were young, did you have a large LP, cassette, and/or CD collection? What format did you begin with? Where is your collection now? Did you have a favorite album cover?
5. Do you play a musical instrument? When did you learn, and how has it served you in life? Have you performed publicly?
6. What are your favorite musical instruments? Why do you like them?
7. What was the first major musical concert you attended in person? What concert did you enjoy most, and why? What was it like to hear a live performance?
8. Have you ever met a famous musician? What were the circumstances? What did you learn from his or her music?
9. In which ways do you think music influences a generation? Can one generation be influenced more than another? Are music of a generation and the time period interrelated?
10. It is said that the music you grew up with during your adolescent years is the music that will stay closest to your heart all your life. Is this true for you? What was the music of your teenage years? Has it remained with you? Do you still prefer it over the music of today?

Legacy Theme 16: My Literary Life

"There are worse crimes than burning books. One of them is not reading them." —JOSEPH BRODSKY

Whether you are reading the morning newspaper or a compelling masterpiece of fiction, you are likely involved with reading, in one form or another, every day of your life. Literacy opens up the world and adds depth, nuance, and understanding to your existence. You make sense of your life and the world through reflective reading. You may seek an escape from your present conditions by entering a novel that transports you to another time and place. One of the greatest quests of humankind is for knowledge, and that often comes from reading. Great literature exposes the fallacies and follies of others and makes them more accessible, more human. Authors such as Chekhov, Eliot, Faulkner, Hemingway, and Poe illuminate the world we live in and help us grow. Contemporary writers, including Mary Higgins Clark, John Grisham, James Patterson, J. K. Rowling, and Nicholas Sparks, entertain us with both realistic and fantastical stories. Think back to your entry into the world of literature. How old were you when you first began to read?

1. You likely learned to read in school, unless an older sibling taught you before then. What were the first books you read in school? Was it easy for you to learn, or did you struggle? What did you feel when you read your first book?
2. What book got you interested in a particular genre (trade fiction, thriller, romance, horror, nonfiction, and so on)? What impact did it have on your life?
3. Often our bookcases are filled with one type of book and few outliers. What genre do you currently enjoy most? Have you changed your focus over the years, moving from one genre to another?
4. Libraries can be inspiring for anyone who loves books. What have been your experiences in libraries? Do you consider yourself a serious reader? If so, who influenced you?

5. Do you read a mix of old classics and new fiction? Are they comparable?
6. Who is your favorite author? What inspires you about this person? Have you ever written to an author?
7. Have you ever belonged to a book club? What was that like for you?
8. Have you ever met a famous author? What was your reaction to meeting him or her in person?
9. Have you written an academic piece of work meant for publication? What was it about, and why did you write it? Have you ever written anything that was published, either in newspapers, magazines, or through a book publisher? Have you written research articles for publication?
10. If you could recommend one book for the next generation, what would you choose? Why? Do you have a list of your favorite books? Do you recommend them to others?

Legacy Theme 17: Greatest Achievements

"To be yourself in a world that is constantly trying to make you something else is the greatest accomplishment." —RALPH WALDO EMERSON

Looking back over your life, it may be difficult to pinpoint your greatest achievements. You might feel that you simply lived your life as best you could at the time, and if you accomplished something, it was a natural outgrowth of your life. You may feel you were called upon to rise to the occasion, to step up to the plate, to stand tall, and you did. At other times, great achievements happened in unexpected ways. You might have been in the right place at the right time to seize an opportunity or accomplish a lofty goal. Later in life, some of these achievements are forgotten or given less importance. Even then, they still give context to your life and who you are now. The achievements you attain are not usually high-profile or top-of-the-news stories. Sacrificing time and effort to become the best possible dad or mom, husband or wife, are earmarks of accomplishment. Serving people in a longtime volunteer capacity is heroic work. Your most commendable achievements can be personal accomplishments that you keep to yourself, or they can be global in scope. Great is great, no matter what. What achievements are you most proud of?

1. What does the term *greatest achievements* mean to you?
2. Childhood is often a time when we are encouraged to try new things. Did you ever win a contest? What was one of your most important childhood achievements?
3. What was one of your most important adolescent achievements?
4. What was one of your most important adulthood achievements? What life lesson did you learn from this challenge that you wish to pass on to your progeny?
5. Did you set your sights on a goal and methodically sit down and plan the steps you would need to accomplish to achieve it? Or did it happen accidentally? What barriers did you face?
6. Sometimes when striving for a goal, we can feel very much alone. Did you have a mentor during the achieving process? Who supported you? What did that give you?
7. Few of us live in a vacuum; rather we have families and responsibilities outside our career. What personal costs might have been associated with an achievement in your field of work? Was it worth it?
8. Were your major achievements generally long- or short-term processes?
9. When you look back on your greatest achievements, how did they help mold you into the person you are today? What are the characteristics necessary for praiseworthy accomplishments?
10. No matter how old you are, there is always room for more achievements. What else would you like to accomplish?

Legacy Theme 18: Courage

"Success is not final, failure is not fatal: It is the courage to continue that counts." —WINSTON CHURCHILL

The direct opposite of courage is fear; without fear, you would have no need for courage. To recall your acts of courage, you need to first examine your fears. Fears serve a purpose in your life. They alert you to potential dangers so that you may act to avoid them. Sometimes you create fears where none exist. Worrying about a future event that you can do *nothing* about only adds stress to your life and weakens your defenses. When you confront your fears and move forward, courage steps in. Think back to times in your life when you were afraid. Were your fears real or imagined? Did they require physical or moral courage? How did you handle them?

1. What recurring fears have you had during your life? Are they primarily imagined fears? The what-ifs of life? What is your first response?
2. You may display courage in many areas of life, e.g., relationships, work, physical or emotional aspects, and so on. Where do you feel you have been most courageous, and why?
3. We all have fears. What persistent fears do you still hold onto in your life? Do you think most people confront their fears courageously? Do you feel you have shown more or less courage as you grow older? What caused this?
4. Courage may be needed for sudden events where quick decisions must be made. Have you ever been faced with a situation where you had to respond immediately with courage? What happened? Did you have time to think, or did you simply act?
5. Who do you consider courageous? Who have been your role models for courage when you were growing up? Were they superheroes or real-life heroes? How did they affect you?
6. What do you consider one of the most courageous things you have done? Did it require moral or physical courage? What happened?

7. In terms of relationships with other people, what is one of the more difficult things you have had to do? What were the short- and long-term implications?
8. Have you ever acted courageously and told no one? How did it make you feel?
9. Have you ever been publicly rewarded for your courage?
10. Have you ever felt personally responsible for falling short of your own definition of courage?

Legacy Theme 19: Cultural Heritage

"As you age naturally, your family shows more and more on your face. If you deny that, you deny your heritage." —FRANCES CONROY

Cultural heritage is comprised of the tangible and intangible artifacts and attributes we inherit from our ancestors and pass on to following generations. This heritage takes two forms: tangible objects such as monuments, books, and works of art, and intangibles such as folklore, traditions, and language. We are all a product of not only our society and upbringing but also the personal cultural heritage that has been passed down in our families. The great majority of us are immigrants or descendants of immigrants. Many immigrated in search of sanctuary and work, while others came under more turbulent conditions, such as war or famine. What is the story of your ancestors? What passed-down artifacts and traditions do you still maintain?

1. What is your ethnicity? What cultural beliefs, values, and behaviors have you inherited from your ancestors? What is your cultural background?
2. Many of us were not fortunate enough to come from storytelling families. What do you know about your ancestors? When did they

arrive here? Why did they come to this country? Where did they first settle?

3. As time passed, did succeeding generations move away from the original geographical area? Where did they settle? Did the new area support their cultural heritage? If not, what did they do to maintain it?
4. Did your recent ancestors experience religious or cultural prejudice concerning marriage and friendships? Is this still the case? How has it impacted your life?
5. We carry our cultural heritage deep in our genetic makeup. Do you still practice cultural traditions from your home country? What are they? If not, why not?
6. What aspects of your cultural heritage do you consider the most positive? Which ones seem less so? How have the traditions changed over the years?
7. Have you visited your home country? Do you still have relatives there? Do you still feel a connection to your past?
8. Is there one family heirloom that you cherish and continue to pass on to succeeding generations? What is the story behind it? Who will receive it when you are gone?
9. What have you inherited from your forefathers that you consider a source of pride? Is it a physical characteristic or an emotional or cognitive factor? Why is this important to you? How does it help shape who you are today?
10. Succeeding generations change as they live through new periods of history and live in a new society. Are there any cultural customs and traditions that you have abandoned as you have grown older? What caused this shift? Do you still feel loyal to your cultural heritage?

Legacy Theme 20: Creativity

"The position of the artist is humble. He is essentially a channel." —PIET MONDRIAN

Creativity is defined as the use of the imagination or the generation of original ideas, especially in the production of an artistic work. Do you consider yourself a creative person? Do you like to paint or draw? Perhaps you enjoy writing or have a green thumb when it comes to the garden. Whatever your creative niche may be, this is the time to explore it. Investigate your creativity and find the ways it is expressed in your life. Talk about your many "works of art," no matter what form they take. Write about your creative process and how it has evolved throughout the years.

1. Thinking back to your early childhood, were you considered a creative child? Were you encouraged to express your creativity in whatever form it took? Or were you discouraged from creative pursuits?
2. Did you participate in activities such as acting, dancing, or singing? Write about that period in your life. Do you still make time for those activities?
3. How do you express your creative urges today? Has this changed over the years?
4. If you do *not* feel creative, what do you think holds you back?
5. Has dance or theater been a passion in your life, whether as an observer or a participant? Have you ever acted in a play? Write about a memorable experience.
6. What was one of the most creative periods of your life? Were you acting in response to the circumstances, or did you initiate the creative process? This involves creative solutions as well as creative acts.
7. Is there one teacher or mentor who inspired you to follow your own creative path?

8. Did you give up early dreams of becoming successful in one of the creative arts? Why, and what impact did abandoning your pursuits have on your life?
9. Though it may not be obvious, cooking, baking and gardening are creative acts. Have you ever improvised and created a masterpiece in the kitchen? Have you planted your own herb garden?
10. As a child, what were you taught about artists and creativity? How has this influenced your life as a creative person?

Legacy Theme 21: Friendships

"I would rather walk with a friend in the dark than alone in the light." —HELEN KELLER

In many ways, your friends have a greater impact than your family. You choose your friends, granting you a freedom that cannot be attained from your more "obligatory" associations with relatives. Friends run the gamut from mere acquaintances to those you can pour your heart out to, and the closest friends accept you no matter what. Additionally, scientists have studied the effect of "confidants" in our lives, and the results indicate that people with confidants have higher well-being. Thinking back, who were your best friends over the years? What brought you together?

1. Have your friends changed over the years? Was there a time that a friend really helped you out that you will never forget?
2. Have you ever had a fight with a best friend? What happened? Did you resolve it?
3. Have you lost a good friend either by moving away or through death? What happened? How did you handle this loss?
4. Did your parents agree with your choice of friends? If not, what did you do? How did this affect you? What did they not like?
5. Are your friends similar to or different from you? Do you think friends must have similar interests and/or moral values to be good friends?

6. What are you prepared to give for a friendship? How much should you compromise your values to maintain a friendship?
7. What do you want most from your friendships?
8. Do you think you can "outgrow" friends? How? What happens?
9. What are the qualities you look for in a friend? Have you ever had a "fair-weather" friend? A close confidant?
10. Do you have one friend who you couldn't imagine being without? What would happen to you? Do you think your spouse can be your best friend? Why or why not? What about your adult child?

Legacy Theme 22: Travels

"There are no foreign lands. It is the traveler only who is foreign." —ROBERT LOUIS STEVENSON

Through your travels, you expand not only your outer world but also your inner one. When you travel to a foreign country, your eyes are opened to new sights of the land, the people, and the culture. You hear new sounds, such as the incessant honking of taxis and wailing sirens in large cities or the hushed whispers of the ocean lapping the shore, punctuated by the cry of gulls. You feel the atmosphere change and become heavier with the humidity and heat or lighter and vaster in a higher altitude. Your palate is awakened by new smells, textures, and flavors of foods never before experienced. Your inner world is shaken by a new reality as you leave your habitual way of living at your doorstep. You step into a new culture with languages, customs, and traditions you may not understand and beliefs that you don't share. Thus you are forced to re-examine your life from a new perspective. You may or may not change, but you will never be the same again. What have been your experiences traveling?

1. Some people begin traveling on family vacations as a child. What are your first travel memories? How old were you? Was the vacation the same every year?

2. One trip may stand out in your memory above the others. What is your favorite travel memory? What made it so significant? Write about that experience.
3. When you travel, do you keep a record for later reference? For instance, do you keep a diary, take photos, and collect souvenirs? What do you do with your memories when you return home? Write about the memories you have collected.
4. Some professions require a lot of travel. Did you travel for your work? How did this change the experience for you when compared to traveling for pleasure?
5. Traveling alone often offers opportunities for meeting others that might not happen in a group. Have you undertaken a major travel adventure alone? Write about the experience.
6. Do you have a favorite travel destination? Have you gone there more than once? Why does it appeal to you? What sights and sounds do you remember?
7. There are many reasons to travel. You may want to visit an exotic culture, swim in warm seas, or view the great works of art housed in museums around the world. What has been your primary motive for travel? How has this changed you? Were your expectations greater than the reality of the trip?
8. What country was so different from your own that you were jolted into a new way of looking at life?
9. At times we may long to travel but don't have the means, and other times we have the means and no desire. Is there a place that you would love to visit but know it will likely not happen? Why? Do you feel you have visited the top ten destinations on your places-to-travel list?
10. What foreign culture interests you, and why? Have you visited this country? How has travel broadened your worldview?

Legacy Theme 23: My Pets

"Until one has loved an animal, a part of one's soul remains unawakened." —ANATOLE FRANCE

Many of us have relationships with animals and pets that extend throughout our lifetime. Your choice of pet is as individual as your personality. Some people are cat lovers, while others prefer the company of dogs. Pets range from dogs and cats to more exotic pets such as snakes, reptiles, and rare birds, and the many benefits of owning and caring for a pet are undisputable. Pets provide companionship, relaxation, and unconditional love. They foster a sense of responsibility and nurturing. Studies have shown that owning a pet lowers blood pressure, diminishes depression, and encourages exercise and social interaction, especially among older people. It is difficult to explain the bond that forms between owner and pet to someone who has never owned one. Have pets been a part of your family? Or have you never owned a pet?

1. The reasons for owning a pet vary with each person. You may have been raised in a family that always had a menagerie of animals and have never considered not owning a pet. Or you may have "married into" a relationship with a pet. What has been your reason for having or not having a pet? Why do you think pets are so important?
2. During your childhood, did your family own a pet? Or were you not allowed to have one? What was that like?
3. Do you have a pet now? What does having a pet mean to you? What does your pet add to your life? If you could have any pet at this time, what would it be?
4. When a pet dies, it is as painful as if we have lost a family member. What has been your experience with the death of a pet? What happened? Have you ever had to have your pet euthanized? How did you manage your grief?

5. We sometimes feel freer and express a different side of ourselves with a pet than we normally exhibit to the world at large. Do you behave differently with your pet than with anyone else? What do you do? How does your pet see you?
6. Have you ever gone through a difficult time when your pet was the support that got you through the crisis? What did your pet do? How do you think your pet knew you were having problems?
7. Families may own a pet, but usually one person becomes the master. How did your pet adapt to family life? Who did it bond with, and why?
8. Our pets often have characteristics and behaviors that make us laugh. What does your pet do that makes you laugh? Has it done something especially funny? What peculiar behaviors does it have?
9. Our pets may also become our teachers. What has your pet taught you? Patience, love, humor?
10. What attributes do family pets have that humans might not?

Legacy Theme 24: Risks in My Life

"And the day came when the risk to remain tight in a bud was more painful than the risk it took to blossom." —ANAÏS NIN

Risk is defined as the potential for damage, loss, or injury weighed against the potential to gain something of value. Everything you do in life involves some risk. Just staying alive involves some risk taking. You take a risk every time you try out something new that could either have a positive or negative outcome. Should you try a new medication on the market even though it has not been thoroughly tested? From your first baby steps to your last breath, you inhabit a world that lurches ahead on uneven ground. You can slip and fall anytime and anywhere.

Most of the world is outside your comfort zone. You can minimize risk by creating and staying within a bubble. Even then, life can trick you; bubbles are fragile.

1. Some people are by nature more cautious and circumspect than others. As a child were you a risk taker and the first one to try something new? Or were you content to let others lead the way? Did you prefer to do things on your own? Did that involve risk taking?
2. Who did you see as a risk taker? Did you have role models in terms of risk taking, whether it was in sports, the arts, business, or real life?
3. Risks run the gamut from tangible to intangible. Are your risk-taking activities primarily physical, emotional, or financial? Did you ever risk your health? What happened?
4. What major risks have you taken? Have you ever lost more than you gained? How have you succeeded?
5. Have you ever regretted not taking a risk? What stopped you? What were the ramifications of not doing so?
6. Does your spouse have the same or different risk-taking interests?
7. Have you ever been in the position of having been forced into a risk-taking situation? What happened?
8. New medications can be risky. Were you ever faced with a disease that required you to decide on a new treatment? How did you weigh the risks?
9. Has your risk-taking behavior changed with age? What is your advice to young people about taking risks?
10. If you are undertaking a new project or aiming for a new goal, what risks are you prepared to take? Do you consider if the risk involves only yourself—or others? Does that make a difference in your behavior?

Legacy Theme 25: Sporting Life

"Sports do not build character. They reveal it."

—HEYWOOD BROUN

Sports have been around for thousands of years. Artifacts unearthed in China indicate sports have been a part of human history since 2000 B.C. Sports were so important to the ancient Greeks that they started the Olympics—the pinnacle of sporting competition. While millions of people participate in sports, millions more are spectators. It is a multibillion-dollar business that consistently fills up stadiums and sends television ratings soaring. Schools and universities support athletic programs, community centers run after-school sports clubs, and pick-up games pop up wherever an open space is available. The benefits of playing sports are numerous: Physical activity is healthy, motor skills are developed, leadership skills are learned, and lifelong friendships are made.

1. As a child, were you good at sports, or were you the last one to be chosen for the team? How did this impact you? What were your favorite childhood sports?
2. Some people seem to be born with a "ball sense" and excel in all sports that include a ball. Do you have any talent for a particular sport? Have you had a lifelong passion for a sport?
3. Do you prefer team sports or solo activities? Do you like to win as a team or on your own?
4. Organized sports are often our first introduction to competition. How competitive are you? How do you react to a personal win or loss? Was there one time when you felt cheated out of a win? What happened?
5. From bull riding to football to running, the level of danger varies among sports. Have you ever participated in a dangerous sport? What was it? Why was this important for you? What did you get from it?

6. Sporting activities not only challenge us physically but also teach emotional lessons of sportsmanship and playing fair. What significance do you attach to the physical and emotional health of playing sports? Is one more dominant than the other?
7. Have you ever won a college scholarship through sports? Where did it take you in life? Have you played a sport professionally? Were you on the varsity team in high school?
8. Football, baseball, hockey, soccer, tennis, golf, and so on all have a wide following of spectators. We can follow our favorite teams and sports figures on television and feel as if we were right there. However the sounds, smells, and feelings when actually attending a professional sporting event in person add another dimension. Have you attended a professional sporting event? Is there one team you continue to follow?
9. Have you ever met a famous sports figure? Under what circumstances? Did he or she live up to your image?
10. As you age, you may need to give up some of your favorite sports due to diminishing physical capacity. Knees give out, and running marathons must be sacrificed to walking. Have you had to quit a sport that you love? How did that affect you? Did you substitute another sport that you are still able to compete in?

Legacy Theme 26: Natural Disasters and Accidents

"Bad things do happen in the world, like war, natural disasters, disease. But out of those situations always arise stories of ordinary people doing extraordinary things."

—DARYN KAGAN

Natural disasters include tornados, hurricanes, floods, earthquakes, tsunamis, and all physical events that have adverse consequences for mankind.

They may leave a trail of destruction in their path and often result in loss of human life and property. Some come with warnings, such as hurricanes, but others, such as earthquakes, simply strike with no chance to escape the devastation. You may have survived unexpected and horrifying natural disasters. Perhaps they have scarred and scalded you, left you in shock, and changed you, sometimes in subtle ways, sometimes for the world to see.

Accidents happen to all of us. They can range from falling and breaking an arm to being the sole survivor of a car accident. Whatever the situation, it is often followed by an emotional and physical fallout. Life is rarely the same afterwards. What has been your experience with natural disasters and accidents?

1. During your lifetime, have you experienced a natural disaster that was so devastating it changed your outlook on life, possibly an approaching fire or flood that had you scrambling for your most precious belongings as you headed out the door?
2. Some people seem to be "accident-prone." Are you one of them? Do you know someone who is? Do you feel that it is possible to bring accidents upon yourself?
3. When faced with an accident or pending disaster, your senses are heightened and you are on alert. Which of the five senses—sight, sound, touch, taste, and smell—stand out for you during a time of crisis? How do they help you cope?
4. Have you ever been forewarned that a disaster was imminent? How did you react as the situation developed? Were you afraid for yourself, your family, others? Were you calm and collected during the crisis or completely frazzled?
5. Accidents and natural disasters often end in a number of losses. What losses did you suffer? Physical property, injury, the death of someone close? What is the worst loss you have experienced?
6. Often accidents end in bodily harm of one kind or another. Were you ever hospitalized due to an accident? What treatments were given to you? What happened?

7. Losses may not only be physical but financial as well. What were the financial ramifications of the incident?
8. Have you undergone counseling because of your experience? Was it beneficial?
9. Did an accident happen to someone who was very close to you that changed your life as well? How has the incident changed you? What happened to your loved one?
10. A tornado may cut a path through a housing tract, leveling one street and leaving the one next to it untouched. Have you ever been the survivor of an accident or natural disaster? What is this like? Do you think you have fully healed?

Legacy Theme 27: Life After Retirement

"Don't simply retire from something; have something to retire to." —HARRY EMERSON FOSDICK

Retirement from the work force is a major transition. Your sense of who you are, your ability to earn money and pay your own way, is drastically changed. Whether planned or unplanned, retirement is transformational. Predictable work routines no longer exist, and the financial impact may force you to budget, perhaps for the first time. Credit and debt management take on new meaning, and estate planning can no longer be ignored. Taxes still need to be paid. Added stress can lead to health implications. Social roles and expectations can shift. Providing for family needs now involves new direction and focus. Maybe it means working part-time or volunteering. Retirement may either be an exciting stage of life or a deeply worrying one. It will always be challenging. What has been your experience with retirement, i.e., either retiring or planning for it?

1. The standard age for retirement is usually sixty-five years. When did you begin to plan for your retirement? Some companies now ask their employees to retire early. Did that happen to you?

2. We all have ideas about what our retirement will be like. For some it may be the possibility of playing golf every day! What were your feelings and thoughts on your first day of retirement? Did that change after a week, a month, or a year? Write about this.
3. The glow of early retirement may seem ideal, but the actuality may vary. While your friends are still working, you are home with time on your hands. Have you taken up new activities or classes? Have you made new friends?
4. Companies today are often downsizing and outsourcing to maintain their profit. If your company downsized, how did this affect you? Did you know it was coming? Could you prepare for it? What did you do?
5. What new daily routines have you developed? How do these affect your partner?
6. What have been the financial implications of your retirement? Any surprises?
7. What lifestyle social changes have you experienced because of retirement? Have you ever felt obsolete?
8. When we meet someone new, the first question often asked is "What do you do for a living?" Now that you are retired, how do you define yourself? Do you feel different? How have you adjusted?
9. Men and women often perceive retirement differently. What has been your experience? Do you feel there are additional challenges based on gender?
10. The major crossroads of life offer you the opportunity to stop, reassess where you have been, and decide where you want to go in the future. After retirement, have you redefined your sense of purpose in life? Where do you want to go in life?

Legacy Theme 28: The Art of Forgiveness

"The weak can never forgive. Forgiveness is the attribute of the strong." —MAHATMA GANDHI

Forgiveness means giving up and letting go of an incident, intentional or otherwise, that caused you personal harm. It does not mean condoning or excusing the offender of the hurtful action but rather that you let go of your anger, desire for revenge, and other negative feelings. There are times in life when people may fail you or vice versa, and the damage can be devastating. It's possible to stay angry and bitter for years. When you refuse to let go, your health suffers. In contrast, forgiving another is empowering. No longer does the other person have control over your emotions. You have symbolically let that person and that issue go. Yet it can be difficult to forgive someone who has wronged you. You may have invested a great deal of time in your anger and even found a sense of tenuous peace in your self-righteousness. What have been your experiences in life regarding forgiveness?

1. Someone may have hurt you intentionally or unintentionally. What happened? Have you found the courage to forgive? What were the circumstances?
2. You might also have harmed someone close to you. Have you ever had to ask for forgiveness? Have you ever been forgiven by another? What did that feel like?
3. When you hold anger or a grudge against someone, it adds stress and anxiety to your life and can take a toll on your health. Research suggests that forgiving someone is healing. Do you believe this to be true?
4. Accompanying the hurt and anger that may arise when someone wrongs you is the desire for revenge. Are you still holding onto a past hurt? Are you ready to give up the desire for retribution?

5. The art of forgiving sometimes doesn't seem fair. Do you feel that it is fair to forgive someone who has hurt you? Can you show mercy to the offender, if not forgiveness?
6. What are your thoughts about forgiving someone who is still hurting you? Do you see it as a sign of strength or weakness?
7. Do you hold the philosophy of forgiving but never forgetting? How has this played out in your life?
8. Forgiveness may also be directed at yourself. Have you ever done something to harm yourself that you need to forgive? Do you believe that forgiveness should be conditional or unconditional?
9. The process of forgiving may be difficult. When trying to forgive someone, were you able to see her point of view, her side of the story?
10. Did you learn a lesson in the process of forgiving? Examples include compassion, patience, and resilience. What have you learned the most about forgiveness?

Legacy Theme 29: Life Miracles

"There are only two ways to live your life. One is as though nothing is a miracle. The other is as though everything is a miracle." —ALBERT EINSTEIN

We use words such as *coincidence*, *serendipity*, *synchronicity*, or *miracle* to help us understand and explain events that seem to happen outside our usual cause-and-effect world. For instance, you might have dreamed about a long-lost friend only to have her call the next day. Or you feel an urgent need to visit someone only to find that you have come just in time to offer emergency help. Synchronicity occurs when meaningful coincidences happen with no logical, explainable cause. In order to detect them in your life, you must suspend disbelief and allow your intuitive self to operate. Some people are more open to miracles than others, but nearly everyone has experienced one. What has been your experience with the unexplainable, synchronistic events in your life?

1. Have you ever witnessed an unexplainable event that could only be described as a miracle? How did it impact your life? What happened?
2. Have you ever witnessed something for which there was no explanation? Did this happen to someone else or to you? Why do you think it happened?
3. We all have an intuitive sense, but some use it more than others. Have you had intuitive experiences during your life? Do they often prove correct? Do they come in the form of dreams or daytime thoughts?
4. Your normal left-brain consciousness can become upset when inexplicable things occur. Are you comfortable with these intuitive situations, or do they create problems?
5. When synchronicities happen in your life, you may feel hesitant to share them with others. You might even have a difficult time acknowledging them to yourself. Is there someone with whom you can freely share the more "out of the ordinary" events in life? Does it help to have someone to talk to about them?
6. Have you ever ignored your intuitions or been persuaded to do so by others? What happened?
7. Have any of your family members or close friends experienced miracles and confided in you? How did you react to them? Did any involve you?
8. Have you experienced a little miracle and never told anyone? If you could experience a miracle today, what would it be?
9. Sometimes people attribute miracles to God. How do you feel about this? How do the unexplainable events in your life influence your spiritual beliefs?
10. Religion and spirituality are both filled with stories of miracles. Do you believe in major historic miracles, such as the first Miracle of Lourdes near Lourdes, France in 1858 and the Miracle of the Sun at Fátima, Portugal in 1917?

Legacy Theme 30: Embarrassing Moments

"Have you ever noticed how parents can go from the most wonderful people in the world to totally embarrassing in three seconds?" —RICK RIORDAN

We have all experienced embarrassing moments in our lives. It may have been something as simple as forgetting someone's name. You also may become embarrassed by the behavior of those closest to you, such as your parents and children. Whatever the occurrence, embarrassment followed because you felt that the behavior or circumstances were inappropriate or socially inacceptable. Along with the feelings of embarrassment are expressions of blushing, sweating, and stammering that often seem to make matters worse. Think back in your life to a time when you longed for the floor to swallow you up and relieve you of your embarrassment. Often these events make for a good story later.

1. Some people seem to attract funny experiences. Are you prone to having embarrassing things happen to you? If so, why might this be?
2. What was the first embarrassing moment that you can remember as a child? As an adolescent or adult?
3. Embarrassments might occur during critical times, such as burping during a job interview or tripping on stage while receiving an award. Were there ever any long-lasting repercussions to an embarrassing moment?
4. What was your most embarrassing moment? Who was there? What happened?
5. What was your funniest embarrassing moment?
6. The embarrassment we feel may be the result of someone else's behavior. Did this ever happen to you? Who was behaving poorly? What did you do?
7. Has the sting of embarrassment faded enough that if you include it in your life story you are comfortable having others read about it?

8. What is your first reaction when you are embarrassed? Do you blush? Do you begin to sweat profusely? Is it always the same response?
9. What is the most embarrassing moment you witnessed someone else experience? How did it make you feel? Was there anything you could do to alleviate the situation?
10. Embarrassments may arise when you do something inappropriate or from some uncontrollable event such as slipping on ice skates and splitting open the seam of your pants. Does the cause of the embarrassment change the feelings for you? Which stories do you tell later about embarrassing times?

Legacy Theme 31: Siblings

"Brothers and sisters are as close as hands and feet."

—VIETNAMESE PROVERB

A sibling is one of two or more people who share one or both parents. Your relationship with your siblings may be one of the longest running relationships in your life. Siblings are typically born within a few years of one another and grow up in the same household. However that does not guarantee similarity, love, and bonding. Sibling rivalry is well known to most parents; a new baby appears and the firstborn is bumped from the number one spot in the family while all the attention is focused on the baby. Brothers and sisters can have such completely different personalities that they question if they are truly related. Growing up with siblings changes your life in ways unique to each relationship. In like manner, growing up as an only child affects your life experiences. Think back to your childhood. If you had brothers and sisters, bring those memories to mind. If you were an only child, what was that like for you?

1. Do you have brothers, sisters, or both? Were you close when growing up?

2. Birth order may have an impact on sibling development. The oldest child is often the most serious and responsible, the middle child the mediator, and the youngest the jokester. If you have siblings, where do you fall in the birth order? Do you see any truth in the generalizations about birth order? How?
3. An only child may feel a responsibility to be everything for the parents. If you are an only child, what was that like for you? Did your parents expect unrealistic things from you? Are you now in a caregiving role for them?
4. When children are born very close together, rivalry may develop as they strive to win their parents' affection. Were you ever jealous of your brother and/or sister?
5. Did your family have a favorite child? How did you know? What was that like for you?
6. Siblings can offer support and comfort to one another when they are growing up. There may be times in your family when your parents fought and you were too young to understand. Did you and your siblings protect each other? If you were an only child, how did you handle stress?
7. Big brothers or sisters may also be bullies, especially if they are given the responsibility to care for the younger children when the parents are gone. Have you ever been teased or bullied by your older sibling? What happened? Did you tattle on them?
8. Fights and arguments can erupt constantly when playing with siblings. Sibling conflicts teach one to compromise and negotiate. You cannot walk away from brothers or sisters and never see them again; they will be at the dinner table when you get home. What was your experience with your siblings and conflict? Was it helpful or harmful?
9. You may have once been an only child, but then your parents divorced and remarried and suddenly you had a houseful of "stepsiblings." What was this like for you? Did you fit in with the new stepfamily?

10. Your brothers and sisters are with you for life. What is your current relationship like with your brother or sister? Are you close? Are there any unresolved hurts and misunderstandings between you?

Legacy Theme 32: The Historical Times of My Life

"Those who do not remember the past are condemned to repeat it." —GEORGE SANTAYANA

As you live your life, history is being made even though you may not be aware of it. In fact, the definition of *history* is the study of past events. Often it is hard to step back far enough to get a historical perspective. As you grow older you have the ability to look back over your lifetime and recall the history that was being played out at that time. For instance, the Vietnam War occurred in the 1960s and 1970s. Depending on where you were, how old you were, and how the war impacted you, your memories of that time will vary from someone else's. If you were born in or before 1955, you likely remember Kennedy's assassination, but your memories of this event will be affected by your age, nationality, and even political persuasion. What major historical events have you lived through? How have they impacted your life?

1. Think back to the year you were born. What great historical events happened during that year? Did any of them directly affect your family at the time?
2. Some families are more political than others. What is the first national election you remember? Do you recall whom your family supported and why?
3. What was the first major historical event that you remembered as a child? How did you learn about it? What did you think of it at the time?
4. Just during the twentieth century our world changed from an agriculture-based society to an industrial one and then entered the information age. What cultural shifts have you experienced from your

years as a child to the present? How have they affected your life? Do you ever long for the "good old days"?
5. Have you witnessed a major historical event firsthand? What sights and sounds do you remember? Was there fear or joy involved? How did you handle that aspect?
6. Is there a particular historical event that affected you the most? Did it inspire you? Did it change your life view?
7. Some of us have played an active role in an important historical period. Did you exert any influence upon any particular historical event?
8. Wars seem to cycle through our lives. Did any war have a major impact on your life? How?
9. Wars can split families as well as countries apart. Have wars and military conflict taken people away from you, or you away from them?
10. Is there any other historical period that you wish you had experienced? What makes you feel a connection with this time in history? Who would you want to be in that time?

Legacy Theme 33: The First Time

"The advantage of a bad memory is that one enjoys several times the same good things for the first time."

—FRIEDRICH NIETZSCHE

Your life is a running history of first times: your first day of school, the first time you stole a kiss, your first speech, your first serious relationship, your first car, your first job, your first trip abroad. Each of us has a surplus of first-time experiences. Regardless of how old you are, these "firsts" are filled with nervous anticipation, excitement, and even trepidation. They often push you outside your comfort zone. New experiences result in new learning, enabling you to attain a broader worldview.

1. Describe one of your very first memories. Why is it significant?

2. When you have a new experience, what emotions are involved? Are you nervous, excited, or afraid? Do you try to avoid new experiences if possible?
3. Some of us are more adventurous than others. Part of this results from how we were brought up. Did your family encourage you to try new things, or were they cautious?
4. Sometimes firsts are connected with age, such as when you are granted your first driver's license or when you are first allowed to drink or vote. Which of these age-related firsts stands out for you? What was your first solo drive like? When did you first taste alcohol? Where were you? What happened?
5. As adolescents, we may fall in and out of love frequently. Who was your first love? How old were you? Describe what happened.
6. Earning your own money is an important milestone. Describe your first paying job.
7. What first experience will you always cherish, and why?
8. If you are a woman and have had children, what was your first pregnancy like? What was it like to have a first child?
9. Not all first times are positive. What proved to be a negative first experience for you? What happened, and what did you learn?
10. The more you experience something, the more competent you become. How does this concept impact your first experiences in general?

Legacy Theme 34: Children and Grandchildren

"Your children are not your children, they are the sons and daughters of Life's longing for itself."

—KAHLIL GIBRAN

This is the opportunity to indulge yourself and write about your children and/or grandchildren. You may focus on the drama of having them as well as the challenges of raising them—and at last, getting to know them as adults. If you do not have children, is there a favorite niece or nephew, or someone else you are close to, whom you could write about? Maybe you have stepchildren? This theme offers you the opportunity to write about your impact on the younger generations as well as how younger generations have influenced you.

1. In what ways has your relationship with your children (younger generations) grown and changed over the years? If you do not have children, why did you decide not to?
2. Describe your relationship with your grandchildren. What would you like to change about the relationship, if anything? Perhaps you would like to spend more time with them, for instance.
3. Do you feel you understand the world young people live in today? What could you do to improve that understanding? Have you ever felt totally out of touch with the life of the younger generations?
4. What are you most proud of about your children? What are you least proud of? What has been your influence in both the good and bad aspects of your children's lives? If you do not have a child, write about the influence this has had on your life.
5. Do you agree with the way your children raise their children? What would you change or do differently?
6. What have been the heaviest responsibilities of being a parent? Of being a grandparent?

7. Do you consider yourself a role model for younger generations? In what way? What is one lesson you would like to impart to younger people?
8. When you hear the adage "blood is thicker than water," what do you think?
9. What are your greatest aspirations for younger generations? What part do you play in assisting them? How would you like to see your family grow and change over the coming years?
10. Thomas Jefferson once said, "The happiest moments of my life have been the few which I have passed at home in the bosom of my family." What comes to mind when you read this quote? Explore your thoughts and feelings.

Legacy Theme 35: Crime and Punishment

"When a man is denied the right to live the life he believes in, he has no choice but to become an outlaw."

—NELSON MANDELA

We live in a world of rules and regulations that guide our behavior and keep our societies functioning. A crime is an unlawful act that is punishable by the state. A variety of crimes can be committed, including crimes against persons, crimes against the state, violent crimes, and white-collar crimes. Legal sanctions are set up by the state to prevent further crimes. Even with all the rules and regulations, no one is perfect. We strive to do our best, but we may fall short even of our own expectations. Think back over the rules that govern your life. Have you ever disobeyed the law because it was against your beliefs or because you were desperate? Did you suffer a lapse in good judgment?

1. Rules are set up for our own protection, but it doesn't always feel that way. Have you ever broken the law—even a minor one? What happened? Were you punished?

2. Everyone has broken a rule at one time or another. This could be something as minor as not returning a library book on time or running a yellow light. Is there one time when you broke the rules that stands out in your mind? What happened? How were you punished?
3. Our original families set the first rules we are expected to follow. Some of us were raised in very strict, authoritarian homes, while others were allowed to do what they wished as long as they did not hurt anyone else. What did you learn about crime and punishment from your childhood? Did you replicate this with your own children?
4. Prisons are institutions where prisoners are incarcerated for major crimes. The logic behind this is that the punishment should fit the crime. What are your feelings about our penal system? Do you feel it prevents crime from recurring?
5. Our personal beliefs may clash with the law. For example, someone may be a conscientious objector and refuse to join the military. Have any of your beliefs been in opposition to societal laws? Have you ever been forced to take a stand on one of your beliefs?
6. Some people join in protests and marches to fight the injustice of current laws. Have you ever joined a group to change the laws of the state? What happened? Would you do it again?
7. Have you been convicted of a criminal offense? How did it happen?
8. Have you ever been imprisoned? What was the experience like? Did you think that the punishment was just? What did you learn?
9. Have you ever been a victim of crime? What happened? Was there successful resolution?
10. Whistle-blowers are people who report misconduct and illegal behavior in an organization. This may entail danger and untold repercussions in their lives. Have you ever reported a crime that authorities did not see? Do you know someone else who has done this? What happened?

Creating Your Own Themes

Your life is unique, and while many of your experiences will be captured in the ten core and twenty-five additional legacy themes, some will fall outside the norm. For instance, you may be a committed environmentalist. It is not your profession, so the Life's Work theme isn't the place for it. However, you feel that your environmental values deserve a place in your life story. Or maybe you would like to elaborate on the wisdom achieved though growing older. That, too, merits a theme. How about your favorite radio and television shows from when you were young? All of these call out for new themes, ones that you can create. Here's how you can do it.

1. What topic do you want to write about? Let's say you wish to write about your concerns for the earth's environment. You could call this theme "Saving Mother Earth."
2. First write a short paragraph that summarizes your thoughts on this topic. Doing this helps clarify exactly what you are looking for and focuses your thinking.
3. Next write a few probing questions to jog your memory. These will help you remember more details regarding your feelings about this topic.
4. Here is what your completed theme might look like.

Theme: Saving Mother Earth

Nature has always played a significant role in my life. My greatest moments of peace and serenity have occurred when I have been camping in the forest, walking along the beach, or riding the ski lift to the top of a mountain. It saddens me to think that mankind is polluting this natural environment to the point that the glaciers are melting and our fish are dying. My goal is to do everything possible to preserve and restore our planet to its natural state.

1. Recycling is one easy way to stop the pollution of our environment. What steps have I taken to make recycling a part of my daily life? How does this help?

2. Planting trees is one way to give back to Mother Earth. What have I done to restore our environment?
3. Environmentalists work politically to pass new laws to prevent the pollution of our country. How have I worked to support this effort? What local clubs do I belong to that work to enhance our environment?
4. Derogatory terms like *greenie* or *tree hugger* are sometimes used to describe environmentalists. Write about the time I was called a tree hugger.
5. What are some of the ways I have changed my lifestyle to decrease pollution? Riding my bike to work is one good example.

Legacy Themes: A Summary

The themes you have written are the heart of your story; they move your narrative forward, keep it in focus, and guide you to the finish line. The result will be a nuanced story of several relevant themes that covers many aspects of your life and does so in a logical sequence. Like an autobiography, it encapsulates a life in all its sweeping contexts, and like a memoir, it focuses on the specifics, discovered through legacy themes. Unlike an autobiography, it is not a linear progression of life events, and unlike a memoir, it does not stay locked into one life theme. Rather it brings into clarity the best of both styles.

PART THREE

TRIM WORK

You are now entering the last few chapters of *Writing Your Legacy.* You have discovered the reasons why you want to capture your life experiences and have learned how to overcome writing obstacles. You have dealt with that nasty critic on your shoulder and entered into the very heart of this book—writing your life story in themes. In Part Three you will add the finishing touches to your life story. You will find chapters on what to do after you've finished writing, how to choose a book title, how to format your book, and how to celebrate its release with family and friends. We have included a Resource section that offers additional information as well as a Life Experiences exercise and a World Events Time Line. Referring to these frequently can add powerful context to your stories.

CHAPTER 24

Adding the Finishing Touches

Plautus wrote, "Let us celebrate the occasion with wine and sweet words." The end of a journey is worthy of all this and more. After all, you have probed deeply into the life you know best—your own—and you have plumbed its depths and searched for meaning. But it was Seneca who wrote, "Every new beginning comes from some other beginning's end." There is more to your story.

Read, Reflect, Revise

If you have followed the suggestions in this book, you have now written a minimum of 7,000 words on the major themes that make up your life. Whether you stopped after writing on the basic legacy themes or continued adding new themes and stories to your life story, it is now time to explore the editing process. Yes, the left side of your brain is now essential in making certain that your writing is clear, expressive, and meaningful. Up until now, we have encouraged you to write freely, spontaneously, and just get the stories onto paper. Now is the time to read and revise them so that what you wanted to convey is indeed what appears on the page. Here are a few suggestions as you begin the editing process.

There are two ways to edit your work: the quick way or the right way. The quick method is to read through your manuscript once, keeping a close eye for detail. Are there misspellings? Do your sentences follow along logically? Do they all lead towards a desired outcome—in other words, are they clearly telling the story you want told? Are there too many long sentences that need trimming?

But this type of surface editing may not produce the results you want. Professional editors often use a three-part system, which includes *developmental editing* (or the ten-thousand-foot view), *copyediting* (or the five-hundred-foot view), and *proofreading* (or the one-foot view). Here's how you can use this method to make your life story the best it can be.

Read your manuscript three times, first from the developmental perspective, then from the copyediting perspective, and finally from the proofreading view. This may sound inefficient, but it actually allows your brain to focus on one editing task at a time. You will more likely find issues that need to be addressed at each level.

Developmental Edit

In this initial read-through, focus only on the big issues. These include the following eight suggestions to guide you through the process.

1. **PRINT OUT YOUR STORIES:** No matter how many pages you have written, it is much easier to work with and read stories when you have a hard copy in your hands. You may have been printing them out all along and have kept them in a folder. Be certain you have all your stories before you begin your review.
2. **READ THEM ALL IN ONE SITTING:** Read through all the stories at one time. Step back and detach yourself enough to read from your intended audience's perspective. As you read, make notes in the margins of the page when something is unclear or problematic.
3. **GET AN OUTSIDE READER:** Find someone whose judgment you trust completely, and ask them to read over the stories for you. Listen to what they tell you, and then make up your mind whether to follow

their suggestions. Remember that it is your story and you have the final say in how it is written.

4. **LISTEN TO YOUR STORY:** Ask someone to read your story to you so that you can hear what you have written. Sometimes hearing it pinpoints prominent mistakes or errors. Reading the work out loud to yourself will also help in this process.
5. **SEEK OUT CENTRAL THEMES:** Each of your stories will have a central theme. Reread what you have written, and make certain everything in a particular story is crucial to that theme. For example, if you have written about the role money has played in your life, the story should focus on one of the many aspects of money, e.g., frugality, saving, spending, and so forth. If you have strayed from the focus and added distracting information on another theme, this is the time to cut it out. Again, keep the tidbits of writing in a separate file for possible later use.
6. **CLARIFY THE POINT OF THE STORY:** Each of your stories will have a beginning, a middle, and an end. Your point is the conclusion. What lesson did you learn? Have you come full circle? If you have not come to a conclusion, add it now.
7. **CUT UNNECESSARY EXPLANATIONS:** Often when we write we think we need to explain every single detail so that the reader will not miss anything. This can be overkill if you constantly find yourself writing explanations of what you are writing. For instance, in one of my classes an older student wrote about Pullman train cars, but none of the younger students knew what they were. Rather than add an encyclopedic description of the history of Pullman cars, she included in her writing her father's duties in his job as a Pullman porter, who the passengers were, the destinations, and so on. This added vibrancy to the story, and the meaning of Pullman cars became evident through the context of the story.
8. **LOOK FOR WHAT MATTERS:** What is the meaning in what you have written? This may be the overarching answer to *why* you have

written your life story. It is the essential part of your story and should not get lost in the details.

Using this developmental editing process will lay the foundation for the second step.

Copyedit

Now you will read your manuscript a second time. You are no longer searching for big problems. Instead you allow your brain to focus only on smoothing out the rough edges. Here's how to do it effectively.

1. **REPLACE GENERALIZATIONS:** Read with a critical eye to discover unnecessary generalizations such as *great*, *nice*, or *wonderful*. Replace these with specific descriptions that show what you are trying to convey. For example we can rewrite "We had a wonderful visit to Paris with our friends Milly and James," to "Our trip to Paris, the City of Lights, rekindled a long-lost relationship with our dear friends, Milly and James." Note how this rewrite also leads us onward—we now want to find out about this relationship.
2. **MURDER YOUR DARLINGS:** This is a phrase many writers are familiar with. It means to get rid of even good writing if it serves no purpose in your story. For instance, you may have written a stunning visual description of a B-52 bomber, but it does not advance your story—it's slowing it down, and a reader might lose interest. There is no reason for this stellar writing in the context of the story you have written. Keep these gems in a file for another story. For now, cut out anything that does not move your story forward.
3. **ADD ACTION:** This may be the time to add movement to your stories by changing some of the general descriptions to action sequences. Use verbs to show what happened and add dialogue as you rewrite a scene of merely descriptors. Let's look at this 'before and after' example.

   BEFORE: Milly and James were our dearest friends. Somewhere along the way, between kids and work, we lost track of them. Then, while in Paris, we stumbled upon them in a restaurant. Talk about serendipity!

AFTER: The Septime lies in the Faubourg Saint-Antoine area of Paris. We love Haute Cuisine, and this little five-star restaurant is bathed in its own reflection, with giant mirrors adding luster to the antique décor. It was through one of those mirrors that we saw Milly and James. They sat across the room at a table for two, a flickering candle casting shadows on their faces. They had once been our dearest friends, inseparable as form and shadow. We had not seen them in fifteen years.

4. **FIX MISTAKES:** When you read over your stories, you will see all the mistakes you overlooked as you wrote and just kept your hand moving. Now is the time to take note and make changes.
5. **TRIM TOO-LONG SENTENCES:** Reading your stories out loud will give you a clear picture of sentences that simply don't work. At times the sentences may be too long and clumsy, or you have chosen a more complicated word rather than the simplest one to get your point across. The way we write reveals who we are and cannot be a facade to hide behind. Write simply and clearly, just as you speak.

Using these ideas will help make your manuscript a smoother read for family and friends. Now you are ready for the third and final editing step.

Proofreading

This is where your eyes and ears are watching for those minute details that can easily escape us. Perhaps a comma is in the wrong place. Maybe a word is misspelled. The proofreading step will capture those errors.

1. **SET IT ASIDE FOR A TIME:** Sometimes we are simply too close to our words and our writing is too meaningful for us to be objective. Give it a rest. Put it aside and read it again in a few days. You may simply need some breathing space before you proofread it.
2. **FOCUS ON THE MINUTIAE:** Watch for misspellings, grammatical mistakes, and typos. Perhaps, within the context of one of your sto-

ries, a maiden name was used in error. Susan Jones is now Susan Thompson. That may or may not be an issue. Double-check for accuracy. Do this throughout your manuscript.

That's it. After reading your life story three times, using the developmental editing, copyediting, and proofreading process, you will turn your stories into a work to be very proud of. You've covered all the bases. Congratulations.

Find the Architecture for Your Life Story House

"Start at no particular time of your life; talk only about the things which interest you for the moment; drop it the moment its interest threatens to pale, and turn your talk upon the new and more interesting thing that has intruded itself into your mind meantime."

—MARK TWAIN

Now that you have written on all the legacy themes that have meaning for you, you are ready to organize them into one logical, coherent life story. Just as there are a number of styles for a house, there are an equal number of ways for you to build your life story. Mark Twain wrote an autobiography that consisted of a series of dinner talks and mirrored the wanderings of the human mind. In like manner, you could simply let your stories stand as you wrote them. We live our lives ordered by time, so a more typical structure for your stories may be chronological. Here are a few suggestions for you to consider as you organize your legacy themes into a complete life story.

Chronological

Time structures our lives from beginning to middle to end. We live from birth to childhood to adulthood and on into old age. These periods could represent sections in your life story, and the themes you have written pertaining to that period would be placed in the corresponding section. For instance, with the "Family" theme, you may have written about your childhood and place in your birth family. Those stories would be placed in the first section, perhaps called "Childhood." However, you may have also written stories about your children and spouse for the "Family" theme. Those stories would be placed in the second section, perhaps called "Adulthood." You can further break down sections based on different periods in life, depending on the stories you have available.

Life as a Giant Oak

Think of your life as a giant oak tree. The roots of the tree contain all your stories about your ancestors: your parents, grandparents, siblings, and the like. They have given shape to the trunk of the oak, which represents you: who you are, your core characteristics, idiosyncrasies, and strengths. The first section would be made up of the ten basic legacy life themes, the first stories you wrote. The branches of your giant oak reflect all that you have done with your life (i.e., having your children, working, earning accomplishments, and pursuing your hopes and dreams), and the corresponding stories should be placed in a second section. Finally, the leaves are decoration, a canopy that covers your oak tree and provides color and character. In the final section you could place your writings about risks, creativity, and all remaining stories.

Let the Themes Guide You

After the first ten core legacy themes, the decisions of which themes to include in your life story is a completely individual matter. Possibly your additional themes focused on people, family, friends, and mentors. If so, you might organize the sections of your life story by the category of people such as ancestors, nuclear family, best friends, colleagues, and so on. The themes you have written are as individual as your fingerprint, and only you can discover an order, an underlying thread that runs through all of the stories. Use this to organize them into a whole.

Understanding Life Backwards

As the philosopher Kierkegaard's quote reminds us, "Life can only be understood backwards; but it must be lived forwards." After reading over all your stories, does a familiar structure become evident? An organic whole should eventually emerge that creates an "a-ha" moment for you. For instance, you may understand for the first time that your entire life has revolved around caring for others. As the oldest child, you were given responsibility well beyond your years to care for your younger siblings due to your mother's illness. When you left home, you continued your caring role as a teacher, a social worker, and finally a hospice nurse. You have always been the caregiver. Realizing this, you can then place your stories within this structure, a framework that takes the shape of an overall emerging theme. Read over all your stories and discover the narrative shape by finding yourself in them.

Let the Chips Fall Where They May

All of your stories are about you and your life. That may be the only organization needed. Your life story may not be a book to be read sequentially, from first page to last, but rather picked up and read at random. You might have a beloved book that you often thumb through, choosing a chapter that offers you solace, an insight, or a smile. This is also how your stories will appeal to your readers. Title each story to reflect the content and attract your readers. Your job is to get the stories out there. It's up to everyone else to read them.

Formatting Tips

Mastering basic word processing skills will help you pull your life story together and make it look professional. You may be familiar with some of these features; others you can learn easily by trial and error or by clicking the "help" button in your word processing program for answers. In addition, there is a wealth of tutorials and assistance to be found on the Internet. Here are a few suggestions to improve the look of your life story. Many of these items can be found on the Home tab or in the formatting or edit menu of your word processing program.

1. **FONT:** Choose a standard font, and use it consistently throughout the text. It is confusing for readers if you change fonts midway through your life story. The standard, easy-to-read fonts that most publishers recommend are: Arial, Book Antiqua, Bookman Old Style, Century, Courier, Garamond, Palatino, Tahoma, and Times New Roman. The standard font size is 12 points, but you may also use 14 to make it easier to read.
2. **COLOR:** There is a palette of hues to choose from if you wish to add a dash of color to your text. This is fun and easy to use, so the best way to learn how to add color is to experiment. One thing to keep in mind: Color adds considerably to printing costs, so use it sparingly.
3. **BOLD, ITALICS, AND UNDERLINE:** These features are used to accentuate words and phrases in the text. For instance, the titles of books are always italicized. You can also choose to underline book titles, but you should remain consistent in your treatment throughout the text. Bold might be used to emphasize the title of your story.
4. **MARGINS:** The standard for most writing is 1-inch margins on all four sides of the paper. If you are planning to bind your life story on single-sided paper, you should leave a slightly larger left margin to accommodate the binding. For example the left margin could be 1.25" while the remaining sides are 1".
5. **LINE SPACING:** Most books are single-spaced, but you may choose to use one-and-a-half- or double-spaced lines.
6. **ALIGNMENT:** Horizontal alignment determines how the text appears on the page. Left alignment is the standard format and means that the left edge of the text is aligned at the left margin. The other options: right alignment (the right edge of the text is aligned with the right margin), centering (each line of text is centered on the page), and justified (the text is aligned evenly on both the right and left margins).
7. **PAGE NUMBERS:** You have the option to print the page numbers at the top or bottom of the page, on the left or right corner or in the

center. By default, in most word processing programs the page number often prints in the bottom right corner.

8. **PAGE BREAKS:** When you come to the end of one of your stories and wish to begin the next one on a new page, use the page break feature found on the Insert tab or menu of your word processor. This will bring you to the top of a new page.
9. **HEADING:** The titles of your legacy stories require a heading to make them stand out. You can do this easily by increasing the font size of the title and emphasizing it in bold. You can also use one of the heading styles on the Home tab or the formatting menu.
10. **EMBED PHOTOS:** Pictures add so much to your stories. If you have scanned your photos into a digital format, it is just a matter of inserting them wherever you choose. Place your cursor where you wish to insert a photo. Click on the Insert tab or menu of your word processing program and pick the option to insert a picture from a file. The picture files on your computer will be listed. Double click on the picture you wish to insert. It will then show up in the text where you had placed the cursor. When the picture is highlighted, you will see a number of creative possibilities open up on the formatting tab or menu. You can wrap text around the picture, add borders, move the picture on the page, resize it, and so on. Experiment with this before you add a photo to your life story. Once you learn how to use this feature, use it often to add a visual element to your narrative.

Legacy Themes as Chapters

When you complete your initial life story writing using the first ten themes, you need to make a decision. "Do I use the themes as chapters? If so, do I label them as such?" No right or wrong answer exists. Naming your first chapter "Forks in the Road" works nicely. Another option is to leave a space between themes but not to name them. This transition effect maintains continuity and flow to your story while moving from one topic to another. If you decide to expand on your life story, perhaps by adding more paragraphs to your initial two-to three-page stories and turning them into longer sections, naming the chapters works well. You may still call the chapters by their themes, but you can also use your imagination. Perhaps your "Forks in the Road" expanded chapter might be called "New Directions" or "Roads Less Traveled."

How to Structure Your Book

Compiling all the essential parts of your book and putting them in the correct order will ensure a professional look for your life story. The following is a list of the standard elements that make up a book. You may choose the ones you feel will add to the readability and presentation of your life story.

- **BOOK COVER:** This is the outside cover of your book. You can simply place your title on the cover or create your own design to grace the cover of your book.
- **TITLE PAGE:** This is the first page of the book. It contains the title of your life story and your name.
- **COPYRIGHT:** This lists the year of publication and your name as the copyright owner. This can be placed on the reverse of the title page, near the bottom.
- **TABLE OF CONTENTS:** This identifies the chapters or sections of your book. If you decide to title each of your stories, those titles would be listed in the table of contents. If your life story is written in sections, e.g., childhood, adolescence, adulthood, etc., the sections would be listed here.
- **PREFACE:** This is a short introduction that discusses your reasons for writing the book.
- **DEDICATION:** This states for whom you have written this book.
- **ACKNOWLEDGMENTS:** This is where you might thank those who have given you support on your writing journey.
- **BODY OR CHAPTERS:** This is the main text of your life story.

- **APPENDIX:** Additional information may be placed at the end of the book, such as resources helpful to the reader. For your life story, you might suggest books and authors who influenced you in your darkest, or perhaps most rewarding, years. You can also include copies of old documents or letters.
- **INDEX:** This is an alphabetical list of significant words and terms found in the book and the corresponding pages.

Now that you have edited the text of your life story so it is clear and concise and created a professional-looking manuscript, there's not much left for you to do except make a trip to the printing office.

Do You Need a Book Designer?

Most of us are not planning to publish our life stories on a grand scale. Our target audience remains our family and friends. However, even within these parameters, book presentation is important. You will want your life story presented in a manner fitting to the tale. Here are five points to consider.

1. A book designer will look at two essential components: (a) cover design and (b) interior design. The cover must be highly visible and attract attention. The inside text must be clear and readable, essentially invisible so that the story stands alone.
2. The cover should reflect the story inside. If your life story is primarily positive in nature, the cover will be the first indicator.
3. The interior design needs to include page layout, type design, and illustration and photo placement. These must all relate to one another in a cohesive and consistent manner.
4. In the commercial world, cover and interior designs generally fall within recognizable templates. Nonfiction books look different than novels. With your life story, you can maintain this professional edge by following these same guidelines.

So, do you really need a book designer? If your intended audience is family and friends, the answer is no—unless you really want to present them with a professional product. Just keep in mind that hiring a designer will likely be expensive.

Spend some time browsing in a local bookstore, paying special attention to book designs. Do you notice a connection between the categories and styles? Pick up a book and hold it in your hands. Does the cover design almost subconsciously tell you that it is a novel, a self-help book, or perhaps a collection of academic research? Is it elegantly presented? If so, then form and function have done their work. Look at a book that is similar to the one you wish to publish. Does it share a related theme? The cover art should reflect that. What about the interior design? Is the typeface easy to read? Are the headings and subheadings logically placed, or do they get in the way of the story? Remember, everything should be as invisible as possible—and by this we mean that no one element should stick out or compete for attention with the actual content. In other words, the story should stand on its own. In the same way, your story needs to reflect you, not someone else's design.

Choose a Title for Your Life Story

"The moment that counts most for me is the one that precedes reading. At times a title is enough to kindle in me the desire for a book that perhaps does not exist."

—ITALO CALVINO

Every life story needs a title because it captures the essence of who you are. Think back to the life you have lived. Does it have a running theme, something that has emerged in the story you have created? Perhaps you have lived a charmed life, teetering along the edge of an abyss but never falling into it. How about the title *Balancing Act*? Or maybe you have faced numerous life challenges, failing along the way but still surviving. How about *My Life: My Nine Lives*? Do you see your life as a tragic comedy? *My Life: Over the Top* might fit. Every life story needs a title. What will yours be?

Brainstorming Title Ideas

Titles can come from the most unexpected places. Here are a few ideas. Take a look and see if any come close to who *you* are. Feel free to use them or let them guide you further into the same line of thinking.

Platitudes can lead to great titles.

PLATITUDE: Good things come to those who wait.
BOOK TITLE: *Good Things Come to Those Who Don't Wait*

PLATITUDE: It could be worse.
BOOK TITLE: *It Could Be Worse—And It Was*

PLATITUDE: Time heals all wounds.
BOOK TITLE: *Time Heals All Wounds—I'm Still Waiting*

PLATITUDE: It is what it is.
BOOK TITLE: *It Was What It Was*

Famous quotations can also lead to interesting titles.

QUOTATION: "If you're going through hell, keep going." —Winston Churchill
TITLE: *To Heaven, Hell, and Back*

QUOTATION: "Only a life lived for others is a life worthwhile." —Albert Einstein
TITLE: *My Life: For Others*

QUOTATION: "As the family goes, so goes the nation and so goes the whole world in which we live." —Pope John Paul II
TITLE: *My Family, My Friends, My Life*

QUOTATION: "In three words I can sum up everything I've learned about life: It goes on." —Robert Frost

TITLE: *My Life: It Goes On* or *My Life in One Sitting*

QUOTATION: "Yesterday is gone. Tomorrow has not yet come. We have only today. Let us begin." —Mother Teresa
TITLE: *My Life: All My Yesterdays*

Here are a few more ideas to consider.

1. Use a phrase from your life story. Often you will have written something that sums up who you are and what the book is about. For example, you might have written, "I shouldn't have been surprised. I waited in that line for three hours before moving to the front of the line, just as they posted the SOLD OUT sign. It's just the way it goes." What a perfect title for someone who lives this sort of life: *It's Just the Way It Goes.*
2. Try a two-word title. Bill Clinton's autobiography is called *My Life.* Frank McCourt wrote *Angela's Ashes.* Even simpler is Margaret Thatcher's *The Autobiography.* How about Walter Isaacson's *Steve Jobs*? Often the most effective titles are just one word. *Night* by Elie Wiesel is one example.
3. Stay away from pompous-sounding titles. *My Life: An Army of One,* comes across as a bit self-serving. *I Did It My Way* is overused and hints of too much "me, me, me."
4. Who will be reading your story? If it's primarily family oriented, with those who know you, try using a catchphrase they will recognize. Do you have a well-used saying? If it's "jumpin' George," an appropriate title would be *Jumpin' George—What a Life.* If you're a person who has her own mind, you might consider *Doing Things Together My Way.*
5. You can choose a subtitle as well. This will further identify what your story is about. *Jumpin' George—What a Life* could be followed with the subtitle *Livin' My Days Away.*
6. What is your story's tone? Is it lighthearted, serious, or documentary-style, where others are interviewed to add balance and perspective to your story? Choose a title that reflects this ambience.

7. You don't need to worry about using someone else's book title. Titles can't be copyrighted.
8. A title is a headline. How many times have our eyes locked on a newspaper or magazine headline featuring the word *secret*? If your life story contains very personal information, call it *My Secret Life* or *Secrets to Tell.*
9. Write down a short one- or two-line synopsis of your story. You might see a title emerging.
10. Use short words with one or two syllables. It may be tempting to use longer words such as *reflections* or *remembering* in your title. However, too many of these will result in an awkward and wordy title, such as *Reflections and Memories of an Accountant's Life. Reflections of a Life* is better, and *The Numbers Man* is best.

You can't always change your life, but you can change the title. Don't be concerned if you have a hard time coming up with one that resonates. It will likely happen at a most unexpected time, just like so many great ideas. A title is the icing on the cake; you can save it for last.

CHAPTER 25

Street Appeal

Deciding on a Final Presentation Format

Despite the old adage, a book will often be judged by its cover—as well as its font style and the way its content is presented. What ultimately attracts readers will be its visual appeal. It looks nice. It feels good in your hands. It holds the promise of a good story within. Perhaps advertising guru David Ogilvy said it best: "A good advertisement is one which sells the product without drawing attention to itself." Now that you've completed your life story, you have two choices. You can tuck the manuscript away, or you can share it with family and friends. If you have written this for others to read, you now need to make it as reader-friendly as possible. You need the gift wrapping that draws them into your story.

Printing

Your last story has been written; you have organized all of the pieces into a coherent whole, formatted the text, and added photos. So what's the next step? Now is when the intangible story of your life that has been living in your computer is transformed into a tangible book to be read and enjoyed by family and friends. You are entering the finishing stages of building your life story. Let's look at a few of the many ways to get your life story in print. You will find a list of websites and information to help you navigate the world of publishing in the Resources section at the end of this book.

1. **PRINT IT YOURSELF.** The easiest method is to simply print out your entire book at home. Depending on the number of pages and the quality and cost-effectiveness of your printer, this is the easiest way to make one copy. You can put the pages into a folder or a three-ring binder. By choosing this method, you can easily assemble at least one copy of your life story for others to read.
2. **TAKE IT TO A LOCAL PRINTER.** There are many local printing services available that will print multiple copies of your life story for you. Just take your print-ready life story to them, and ask for printing quotes. They will ask for it in a PDF format so that no printing errors occur. Whatever you have in the file is exactly what will be printed. Most services offer a selection of binding services that include comb binding, spiral binding, perfect binding (as in a paperback book), and some may even offer hardcover binding. The prices will vary by the number of pages, and you may be required to order a minimum number of copies. This is an option you will need to explore yourself.
3. **BUY YOUR OWN THERMAL BINDING MACHINE.** Thermal bookbinding machines are relatively simple to operate, and the cost ranges from $500 to $1,000. The basic principle is simple: The spine of the book cover contains a thread of glue, the pages of your life story writing are placed inside the cover, the book is then secured in the thermal element for a minute, and voilà! After a short cooling period you have your own hardbound book. The costs not only include the equipment, but you will also need to carry an inventory of book covers based on the width of the spine (number of sheets of paper it will hold) and color. This may be a good option if you are planning to print many books. It is worth investigating.

4. **PRINT-ON-DEMAND.** A quick search on the Internet will yield a number of companies that allow you to build your own book and print it one copy at a time. Each has its own software program and templates to help you create a book to suit your individual needs. You choose your own book layout and design, complete the project in your own time, place your order, and the books will be shipped to you. Depending on your skill level on the computer and your ability to work with book design software, this is a popular option for many people who plan to print only a few books. The cost will vary by the number of pages, number of photos, etc. You are able to print one book at a time if you choose, so there is no need to warehouse extra copies of your book.
5. **SELF-PUBLISHING.** This option is a great idea if you want to print a number of books to be read by family and friends. It's a streamlined approach that excludes agents and publishers and lets you control the entire process, from editing, font choice, and cover design to distribution. The price will always depend on how elaborate you wish to make the book and how many copies you wish to produce. An Internet search will quickly reveal the many bookmaking services that are now available. Just as memoir writing has increased in popularity, so has the business of printing the memoirs as books for family and friends. Keep in mind these important points when working with a bookbinding company.
    - They print and bind exactly what you send them. If there is a typo, it will be printed. You need to have your life story in print-ready format, usually as a PDF file.
    - Unless you are very good with design and book layout, you will need a book designer to help lay out your book for you. Often the printing company offers this service for an extra charge.
    - Ask for and review a sample of the book manufacturer's work before you make a final decision.

- Check whether they have in-house printing capabilities or if the books are sent to an outside printer. Outside printing usually increases the cost.
- Always read the fine print in the contract. Check if there will be sales tax and shipping costs added to the total. Confirm the delivery date.

It may feel like a giant leap of faith to send your precious life story through cyberspace to be printed, but you will forever treasure your life story book when you hold it in your hands. Many companies offer deluxe services that can turn your story into a treasured heirloom. The end product is high quality, meant to last for generations.

A more recent innovation is digital publishing. By e-publishing, you can produce and sell digital copies of your work, bypassing some—but not all—of the publishing roadblocks. If you are computer savvy, this is an option worth considering.

Publishing Options

TRADITIONAL

An author is "contracted" by a publishing house to publish his or her book. The publisher owns the rights to the book and prints, publishes, and sells the book for the author, who receives royalties.

SELF-PUBLISHING

The author pays for the editing, book design and layout, and formatting. There are some self-publishing companies that offer editing and book design services for an additional fee. In this case, the author finances all the costs and owns the rights to the book.

PRINT ON DEMAND (POD)

For authors who need only very small quantities of books for family and friends. As with all self-publishing, the author is responsible for all the costs and editing services. A single copy may be printed in color, perfect-bound, and shipped to the customer.

PRINT SERVICES

- **BOOK1ONE (BOOK1ONE.COM):** Book1One is located in New York and has been offering printing and binding services to writers and authors since 2005. Their binding services include hardcover, soft cover, saddle stitch, coil, etc. They are reasonably priced and will print from one copy to thousands in black and white or color. They do not offer editing services and print only from PDF files.
- **ANGEL PRINT (ANGELPRINT.COM):** Angel Print offers both digital and offset printing from their location in San Diego County. Their services include both full color and black-and-white printing with no minimum order. No editing services.

WEBSITES

- **UBUILDABOOK (UBUILDABOOK.COM):** This company offers short runs of one to one thousand copies, custom covers, standard or custom sizes, and seven- to ten-day turnaround time.
- **BLURB (BLURB.COM):** This independent publishing platform gives you the ability to create, publish, sell, and distribute photo books, trade books, and magazines in print and digital formats.
- **LULU (LULU.COM):** Lulu's services include soft or hardcover books, black-and-white and color printing, and choice of bindings and size.
- **IUNIVERSE (IUNIVERSE.COM):** This company offers a variety of editing services and self-publishing book packages.
- **OUTSKIRTSPRESS (OUTSKIRTSPRESS.COM):** This self-publishing company provides full-service support, writing, and marketing services.

Professional Publication

The vast majority of life stories written today are meant for a select audience of family and friends who will cherish your work long after you are gone. However if you have an extraordinary tale to tell and wish to share it with the world, you may decide to approach a traditional publisher. There are many hurdles to overcome since publishing is a business and manuscripts are only acquired if they have the potential to make money. In most cases, a literary agent is necessary to publish in the traditional realm, and it may be difficult to acquire. However, we all have unique stories, and if one resonates with an agent, the road to getting your work published will suddenly be a bit easier to navigate.

How do you land an agent? Several books will show you how—two excellent ones are Chuck Sambuchino's *Get a Literary Agent: The Complete Guide to Securing Representation for Your Work*, published by Writer's Digest Books, and *The Complete Guide to Hiring A Literary Agent* by Laura Cross, published by Atlantic Publishing Group, Inc. Your agent will then be responsible for placing your manuscript with an appropriate buyer (a publisher).

Should your work be accepted, the publishing time line is typically about one year—and sometimes longer. During this time, your book will be edited for content and structure, designed, proofread, and printed. Once it is released, an in-house publicist will work to market your book.

Traditional publishing does not cost you any money since the publisher makes a profit from book sales. In most cases you are paid a royalty and sign over the rights to your book to the publisher. You may also receive an advance against royalties that is paid up front, before the book is published. This advance does not need to be paid back, but you must first "earn out" your advance in book sales before you receive additional royalties.

Numerous small presses do not require a literary agent for submissions. You submit work directly to the publisher, but only after sending a query letter. There are several excellent books on that topic, one of the best being *The Writer's Digest Guide to Query Letters* by Wendy Burt-Thomas. An excellent free alternative is to check the Writer's Digest website (www.writersdigest.com) and type *writing a query letter* into the Search box. It will take you directly to the information you need.

Strengthening Your Author Platform

You've written your life story. You've edited and assembled it into a compelling narrative. Now a family member or friend is encouraging you to take the next step. *Get your story published so the world can read it.* Is that possible? Does an outside market exist for an ordinary person's life experiences? Would anyone beyond your immediate circle be interested enough to pay money to read it? Would an agent or publisher be willing to take a chance?

In the good old days of publishing, the first priority was a great story, something that would resonate with the average reader. It was easy to browse bookstore shelves and find autobiographies and especially memoirs, often by not-so-famous people. That's no longer the case. The majority of titles are celebrity driven. Just check any tabloid front page—these are the people who get their stories told. So, how do you get yours out there?

One time-tested solution stands above the rest: You start small and aim higher. Each of your legacy stories is the perfect length for submission to any number of local or regional newspapers or online news magazines. Take the time to research the possibilities, find out which editors or publishers are willing to accept human-interest stories, and start there.

Reality Check

If you have written on the ten core legacy themes, you will have created a document of about 7,000 to 8,000 words. The typical published autobiography or memoir in a bookstore runs from 60,000 to 80,000 words. Simply put, you will need more material to traditionally publish your life story. Only by enhancing the ten core legacy themes and/or by adding several of the optional themes will you create a minimal life story manuscript that might interest publishers.

Personalizing Your Author Platform

If you are serious about building your readership, here are three steps to consider.

1. Begin by localizing. You need to become a player in your community, someone with name recognition. The logical way to do this is to become an expert in your field and to get that message out. What are you an expert in? You've written your life story, and that makes you an expert in life. You are a survivor, and so is everyone else. You can assume a leadership role by telling your story through the local media. Newspapers, radio, and television are always open to human-interest stories, especially during family-oriented times such as Thanksgiving and Christmas. Take a look at your life story. Would others learn from it? Does it strike a universal chord?
2. Contact local clubs and community agencies for speaking opportunities. Rotary, Kiwanis, and Chamber of Commerce groups are often looking for people to talk about relevant topics.
3. Create a social media presence. This includes developing an e-mail list, writing a blog, contributing to other blogs as a guest, creating a Twitter account, and using Facebook and similar applications. None of these alone will create the spark you need to become recognized. Combine them with lots of old-fashioned promotional footwork—and you might have a winning strategy.

Check the Internet for lots of free material on creating your own author platform. Or read Tim Grail's *How to Sell Your First 1,000 Copies* and *Create Your Writer Platform* by Chuck Sambuchino. Both are published by Writer's Digest Books and are two excellent books worth their weight in gold. To learn how to become media savvy, set aside time to read *Step Into the Spotlight!: A Guide to Getting Noticed* by Tsufit, published by Beach View Books.

Create Your Life Story in Video

An alternative to writing your life story is to video record it. Today there are many professional services that offer this method of capturing your memories. Videographers will build a story around your life and record it. They will intersperse shots of you sharing memories with photographs and memorabilia. The result can be a professionally edited home movie.

You may choose to video record your story on your own. There are many do-it-yourself tools available to help you in this process. You can adapt the legacy themes and questions to your video. Just as a scene is to a movie, a theme is to your life story. For instance, you want to tell people about your travel experiences. *Travel* is one of many additional themes you will find in this book, and you can use the questions as you plan out your script. Here are some of the steps you need to follow in order to video record all or part of your life story.

1. **COLLECT THE NECESSARY EQUIPMENT:** You will need a digital camcorder, a tripod, a good microphone, a scanner for photos, and a computer with video-editing software.
2. **OUTLINE YOUR SCRIPT:** Choose the legacy theme you wish to start with. For example, you may choose the Travel theme. Look at the probing questions, and think about those that resonate with you. Write up a short outline of the points you wish to cover with each question.
3. **SCOUT A LOCATION:** Find a comfortable, quiet place to record, and consider it your set. It could be your kitchen table or an easy chair in your den. Make sure it is uncluttered since the focus needs to be on you, the subject.
4. **FIND A PARTNER:** You will need someone to work with you on your video. It could be as simple as having a friend who is familiar with video recording start and stop the camera for you. This person will be your assistant when you are in front of the camera.
5. **START RECORDING YOUR STORY:** When the camera starts rolling, you should be ready to discuss the first prompt on your script outline. If you're starting with the "Travel" theme, this would be, "What trip

stands out in your mind, and why?" Let's say you chose your visit to Hoover Dam. You might say, "Walt and I visited the Hoover Dam site while we were vacationing in Las Vegas. The mass of concrete, steel, and water left us in awe. We even had the chance to go deep into the very heart of the interior." This does not need to be written out since the prompt, Hoover Dam, will start your memories flowing.

6. **STOP THE CAMERA BETWEEN QUESTIONS:** You can stop the camera after each question to glance at your script and prepare for the next recording. That will keep you from "reading" your notes in a wooden or monotone way.
7. **MORE QUESTIONS:** If you wish, you can add more to the Hoover Dam segment, or you can choose a few more travel-related questions from the theme list. Go over your script point by point.
8. **INCLUDE PHOTOS:** To make your video compelling, you may insert photos—either digital or scanned—to fit the story you are telling. Your movie software can guide you through the process. For example, you might have mentioned seeing nearby Lake Mead. You would insert that photograph, or series of photos, after you have reminisced about it.
9. **ADD ADDITIONAL SEGMENTS:** When you are finished with each question, you will have a running video that opens with a particular trip, followed by related photographs. You will continue with another probing question and insert appropriate photos until you feel that you've completed this theme.
10. **ADD ADDITIONAL THEMES:** Choose another theme to add to your video, and follow the same steps you used for the "Travel" theme. Keep your videos short. Each theme will cover about five minutes of video time. If you have decided to include just the ten core legacy themes, your finished video will be about fifty minutes long. Your audience will be more comfortable watching a well-edited short production than a ninety-minute documentary.

11. **ADD SOME MUSIC:** With a bit of practice, you can add music to your video, running it softly in the background when you are talking and increasing the volume when photos are displayed.
12. **TITLE YOUR VIDEO:** Choose a title for your mini-production, as well as end credits.
13. **SAVE THE END PRODUCT:** Finally you can save your movie in various formats. You can also hire a company to produce multiple physical copies for you.

If this process seems overwhelming, you can hire a local production agency to assist you. Better still, the creation of amateur videos is a popular activity, and many people are familiar with it. Ask your neighbors and co-workers if they can assist. One of them may have a computer-savvy relative or friend.

Remember: It's your memories, your vision, and your production. Let others help take you there.

CONCLUSION

Preparing Your Open House

Uncorking the Champagne

Life is like riding a bicycle. To keep your balance, you must keep moving. —ALBERT EINSTEIN

You have spent days, weeks, months, and maybe even a year writing your life story, and now it's finished. You've assembled the pages, edited and added photos, and given it a title. To truly set it apart, you have designed a book, either self-published or simply bound. What's next? We mark significant moments in our life with rituals, ceremonies, and celebrations. The completion of your life story is a significant moment and deserves to be recognized in some way. If you have written primarily for your family, plan a family get-together—a book signing party—when you will give copies of your book to those you love. If you've written for distant friends and colleagues, prepare a cover letter and mail signed copies of your book to them. Possibly you plan to donate one to your local heritage society or library; they will be pleased to receive a copy. These are just a few examples of the journey your book may take. Ultimately, it will have a life of its own.

Whatever you choose to do, the important point to keep in mind is that *you* did it! You weathered the storms of doubt, fear, and uncertainty that may have plagued you along the way. You built your life story, word by word, and now hold the completed version of your life legacy in your hands. Congratulate yourself—celebrate yourself! You have left the cherished gift of your legacy for posterity. As Jim Birren always reminds his students, "Onward!" You still have years to live and will have more stories to write.

A Few Last Words

There. You're done. You've read the book and have perhaps completed the core themes and exercises. Or you've read the book and are now all set to take the writing plunge. Remember, *Writing Your Legacy* is your life jacket. It can keep you afloat through the muddy waters of your past. We are all survivors in this world. We have our stories to tell. It is our hope that you embrace your own courage and fortitude as you embark on this greatest of journeys: capturing the life you lived and sharing it with others.

—Cheryl and Richard

Resources

You have now learned how to write your life story using legacy themes. Here is some additional information that may reinforce your learning and add to what has been covered thus far.

Appendix A: How to Create a Successful Legacy Writing Club

Writing is a solitary effort. It can get lonely trying to find the words and sentences that bring your life into new focus. Sometimes, family members are too close and might not be supportive. A great solution is to create a legacy writing club.

Book clubs are a popular venue where people gather in cozy groups to discuss a selected book. One of the members takes the lead and facilitates a comfortable daytime or evening meeting. He or she will greet guests, offer light refreshments, and introduce the topic of discussion. A few hours later, a new book is assigned for reading, and a meeting date is scheduled. The only continuous cost might be the purchase of the book.

Some book clubs fizzle out after a few weeks. Others, the serious book clubs, may last for years, cover numerous books, invite selected authors for guest appearances, and even record meeting minutes.

The same format can be applied to a Legacy Writers' Club; the members will be supported and encouraged as everyone writes their life story. Instead of discussing books, you write and share stories about your life, the one you know so well, the one that offers laughter and tears and may offer important lessons to others. Other members of the club share their stories in turn.

A Typical Legacy Writers' Club Meeting

The Booker Valley Legacy Writers' Club meets once each month. Laura is hosting this evening, and she has arranged for a few light refreshments. The four members arrive at 7 P.M. and gather around the table. Greetings are exchanged, and Laura starts the meeting. Each guest has written a two- to three-page story on "My Family, My Self," a theme that was assigned at the end of last month's get-together. Laura reads her story first. The group then offers supportive comments: "You have such wonderful children." "I love the way you handled her illness." "I admire your courage." No judgments are made. No solutions are offered. The atmosphere is one of acceptance. Laura keeps track of the time—each person is given fifteen minutes to read a story and listen to comments. When the five family stories are shared, including her own, she introduces the next theme, *The Meaning of Wealth*, and the meeting winds down.

Five Steps to Beginning Your Own Legacy Club

1. **GET THE WORD OUT.** Think about your friends. Which ones might be interested in writing their life stories? If you are a Baby Boomer, your peer group will be especially curious. Many will have adult children and grandchildren with whom they will want to share their stories.
2. **DECIDE THE GROUP'S SIZE.** The ideal size for the club is five to six members. This gives each participant adequate time to share their story. Caution: Group dynamics can play an important part in creating a strong and lasting Legacy Writers' Club. You should consider the reason each member wishes to be part of the group. Is it primarily a social occasion, or do they want to discover more about themselves? You need to stress the importance of commitment and

continuity with the group. Once the participants have started sharing their stories, it is not a good idea to add a new member. This can disrupt group bonding. New members can always be encouraged—the ideal time is after the initial ten themes have been covered.

3. **DECIDE HOW IT WILL BE HOSTED.** The host takes on the responsibility of facilitating discussion. This may include keeping members on-topic and providing the writing theme for the next meeting.
   - **TIME:** Arrange a set meeting time on either a weekly, biweekly, or monthly basis.
   - **SPACE**: How much room will you need? An ideal location is the kitchen or dining room table. Members will have sheets of paper and a space upon which to write notes.
   - **LOCATION:** The easiest way may also be the fairest. Each member hosts an evening in his or her home.
4. **ESTABLISH GROUP GOALS.** Consider these three important points when establishing the group, before the first meeting starts.
   - **CONFIDENTIALITY:** Sometimes a story may reveal personal information that needs to stay within the room. No one should be pressured to reveal more than they are comfortable sharing. When each member first joins the group, he or she can sign an informal contract, which will serve as a reminder of the importance of confidentiality. It may not be legally binding, but it is nonetheless a reminder of the importance of discretion and privacy.
   - **ACTIVE LISTENING:** We all like to be heard. Active listening is listening with intent—really hearing what the speaker is saying. Often, when we should be listening to the other person, we are lost in our own thoughts, thinking about what to say next.
   - **SUPPORTIVE, NONJUDGMENTAL COMMENTS:** We have all done things we may not feel proud of, even though they help us learn right from wrong. The hardest lessons may be the most important ones. Occasionally you might hear a story involving a poor decision that resulted in embarrassment or tragic

consequences. It is not your place to offer advice beyond simple acknowledgment that you have heard the story and understand the pain it may have caused.

Statement of Confidentiality and Attendance

Each person participating in this group is honored with mutual respect as we share personal experiences and memories.

I pledge to hold all information shared in this group setting in strict confidence, and I trust that each person here will hold information I share in the same manner.

I will attend all meetings unless there is a serious conflict. In that case I will contact the guest host to make arrangements for my absence.

____

Signed Date

5. **DEVELOP A MEETING AGENDA.** How do you begin each meeting? What happens during it? How does it end?
   - **HOW DO YOU BEGIN EACH MEETING?** Once the members are gathered around the table, the meeting begins with a simple statement such as: "This evening we are meeting to share and discuss our life stories on the theme "My Life's Work." We will take turns reading our stories, followed by short comments. Lynn, would you like to start first?"
   - **WHAT HAPPENS DURING THE SESSION?** When a person finishes reading, often there will be silence. People will be waiting for someone to comment. As host, you can always say, "What a powerful story. Does anyone want to comment on it?" That will open the floor to discussion. Be mindful of time. Allow a few moments for conversation, and then move on to the next reader. "Thank you, Lynn. May we hear yours next, Christy?"

Because each story may take several minutes to read and comment on, it is a good idea to break for refreshments after the first three people have read their themes.

- **HOW DOES IT END?** Once all of the stories have been read, it is time to assign the next life story theme. The first ten should reflect the sequences shown in this book, starting with "Forks in the Road" and ending with "My Legacy Letter." Each theme has a description and probing questions that can be reviewed with the group. The final decision will be who hosts the next meeting.

Tips and Ideas

- Give your Legacy Writers' Club a name. It can reflect the area you live in, e.g., The Elmdale Legacy Writers' Club. If you are unsure of a name, think about what the members have in common. Are they all over sixty? How about The Boomers Legacy Writers' Club? Is it just a guys' church group? Men of St. Paul's Legacy Writers' Club might work.
- A Legacy Writers' Club works with any combination of members: one or both genders, young and old.
- During the first meeting, ask each participant these questions. "Why are you here? Who are you writing your life stories for?"
- In every group one person tends to dominate and take over a conversation, turning the focus back to his or her personal issues. There is no easy way to stop this without causing a rift. Experienced facilitators manage this disruption by waiting for a slight break in the conversation, perhaps a sentence ending, and interjecting with, "Those are good points. Emily, would you add to that?"
- Should there be a weekly charge? If all meetings are held at one person's home, then it's reasonable to charge a small fee to cover refreshments. If the meetings will alternate between members' homes, this fee is unnecessary. A free-for-all policy works best. One option is to collect weekly dues for use as a group contribution to a nonprofit.

Sometimes even a token, monetary investment will ensure commitment from the members.

- Where do you find the writing themes and handouts for participants? Perhaps the handiest source will be this book. It contains everything you need.
- What if someone can't make it to a meeting? They can still write their two- to three-page story and have another member read it. Perhaps this responsibility could fall upon the host.
- If a reader is reluctant to share part of a story, no adverse pressure should be applied. The reader will read only what he or she chooses.
- Any group process can lead to a healthier lifestyle. It is important to remember, however, that though this may be therapeutic, there is no intent to change a person's behaviors. It is not therapy.
- Once the ten core themes are covered, what happens next? Does the Legacy Club end? There are many additional themes to use, all of which are included in this book. Participants may also wish to expand upon earlier themes, turning them into longer stories.

Spending time with others who are writing their life story can be a rewarding learning experience. It may bring people together who might not normally cross each other's paths. It can result in new perspectives in thinking. It can add a mixture of laughter and tears, the great cauldron of social bonding. Best of all, it's fun.

Appendix B: Life Experiences

Here's an incredible fact: You have experienced the world in a different manner than anyone else. If you have yet to be convinced, try this exercise. Here are 303 life experiences divided into categories such as Adventure, Career, Learning, and Travel. Read through them, ticking off ones you have personally experienced. Pay attention to ones that spark strong memories. A story is hidden there, waiting to be written.

303 Life Experiences

Adventure

__ Elope in Rome
__ Own a motorcycle
__ See an iceberg
__ See a glacier
__ Ride a monorail
__ Ride a subway
__ Ride in a double-decker bus
__ Ride a jet boat
__ Ride a kayak
__ Ride a hovercraft
__ Ride in a hot air balloon
__ Board a supertanker
__ Ride in a tugboat
__ Climb a significant mountain
__ Drive a motorboat
__ Jet ski
__ Drive a snowmobile
__ Swim in a high surf
__ Skinny dip
__ Ride in an army tank
__ Fly in a helicopter
__ Board a nuclear-powered ship
__ Board an aircraft carrier
__ Board a submarine
__ Fly in a jet fighter
__ See actual moon rocks
__ Experience gravitational weightlessness
__ Ride a roller coaster
__ Go down a high water slide
__ Touch or pet dangerous wildlife
__ Ride an elephant
__ Ride a horse
__ See a whale
__ Swim with the dolphins
__ Dangle on a rope from a helicopter
__ Drive a bulldozer
__ Visit a war zone
__ Explore a large cave
__ Walk through a jungle
__ Fly in a seaplane
__ Climb an oil storage tank
__ Participate in a parade
__ Hitchhike between towns
__ Ride in back of a pickup truck
__ Ride in a semitrailer
__ Hitch a ride in a boxcar
__ Jump off a five-meter diving board
__ Go down the up escalator
__ Panhandle
__ Gamble in a casino
__ Climb a fire tower
__ Experience virtual reality

Careers, Jobs, and Work

__ Have the perfect job
__ Perform shift work
__ Be the boss
__ Hire or fire someone
__ Work in a hospital ER
__ Perform heavy manual labor
__ Be self-employed
__ Become a board member
__ Become president of an association
__ Work two or more jobs at once
__ Receive a job-related award
__ Join a task force
__ Have an office romance

Creative

__ Write a screenplay
__ Write a stage play
__ Write a radio drama
__ Create a love poem
__ Write a love letter
__ Write a letter to the editor
__ Win a literary competition
__ Get published
__ Write a novel
__ Write a novel on a South Pacific island
__ Begin a journal

Culture

__ Drive a luxury vehicle
__ Ride in a stretch limousine
__ Drink an expensive wine
__ Live abroad
__ Dine in a castle
__ Know people from around the world
__ Live in a culturally diverse neighborhood
__ Work in a culturally diverse workplace
__ View original works of art by famous artists
__ Be part of a professional film production
__ Attend a professional stage show
__ Attend a book reading
__ Own an original Picasso sketch
__ Have a self-portrait made
__ Visit a refugee camp
__ Speak two or more languages
__ Meet a successful author

Events

__ See a U.S. President
__ See the Queen
__ Shake hands with a national leader
__ See a foreign leader
__ Shake hands with royalty
__ Talk with royalty
__ Attend a massive outdoor concert
__ See the northern lights
__ Experience an earthquake
__ Experience a hurricane
__ Experience a tornado
__ Experience an eclipse of the sun
__ Own a piece of the Berlin Wall
__ See a shooting star

Family Matters

__ Be happily married
__ Purchase a home
__ Own a cottage
__ Have a daughter
__ Have a son
__ Have twins
__ Experience or witness childbirth
__ Cultivate relationships with relatives
__ Research your family tree
__ Write your life story

Financial

__ Create a budget
__ Win over $100 in a lottery
__ Put ten percent of your salary in savings
__ Invest in stocks and bonds
__ Lose money in the stock market
__ Loan money to someone

Health

__ Lose 50+ pounds
__ Have major surgery
__ Have a professional massage
__ Experience reflexology
__ Attend yoga classes
__ Have physiotherapy
__ Stay healthy
__ Walk long distances
__ Be hypnotized

Hobbies

__ Become an authority in a chosen hobby field
__ Begin a coin collection
__ Begin a stamp collection
__ Design and build a workshop
__ Fly a kite
__ Build a model railroad village
__ Grow a garden
__ Own a chainsaw
__ Make money from a hobby

Learning/Education

__ Obtain a university degree
__ Get an A+ in a college class
__ Make the Dean's List
__ Create and teach a course
__ Learn a new language
__ Learn a martial art
__ Learn to drive a standard transmission vehicle
__ Master a video game
__ Learn how to cook
__ Be computer literate
__ Understand the stock market
__ Build a website
__ Learn how to juggle
__ Learn to ballroom dance
__ Learn to sail

Music

__ Play a musical instrument
__ Learn to read music
__ Own a digital keyboard
__ Own an expensive guitar
__ Attend a symphony performance
__ See a favorite musical act
__ Have a backstage pass for a major musical act
__ Get a rock star's autograph
__ Compose music
__ Jam with a band
__ Play in a band

Personal Development

__ Take more chances
__ Dislike no one
__ Improve memory
__ Remember peoples' names
__ Become more self-confident
__ Improve lateral-thinking skills
__ Be more disciplined
__ Be more assertive
__ Have better leadership skills
__ Overcome hardship
__ Conquer an addiction
__ Find true love
__ Fall in love hard
__ Join Toastmasters
__ Conquer fear of speaking in public
__ Be arrested for a noble cause
__ Be a mentor to someone
__ Succeed or fail in life with grace
__ Help others
__ Know what it is like to love, lose, and grow from it

Social

__ See Third World poverty up close
__ Have lasting friendships
__ Have special friends of both sexes
__ Advocate for children in society
__ Be a dinner speaker
__ Receive a standing ovation
__ Run for political office
__ Reconnect with first best friend
__ Meet a millionaire
__ Meet a billionaire
__ Correspond with a famous star
__ Send a message in a bottle
__ Taste the perfect chocolate chip cookie
__ Create your own secret recipe
__ Go on a shopping spree
__ Attend a press conference
__ Meet an influential person
__ Speak to an astronaut
__ Take part in a demonstration
__ Sit on a jury
__ Live on all sides of town
__ Be interviewed on radio
__ Be interviewed on television
__ Go to a drive-in theater
__ Have a dog/cat/bird
__ Own a convertible
__ Own a sports car
__ Own a vehicle for every day of the week
__ Own a fine wine
__ Grow a beard or moustache
__ See a Nobel Prize winner

Spiritual

__ Donate a large sum of money to a charity anonymously
__ Have a prescient dream
__ Attend Muslim-Jewish-Christian ceremonies
__ Walk on fire
__ Hug a witch
__ Grow in faith
__ Forgive another
__ Do the Twelve Stations of the Cross in Jerusalem
__ Attend a human birth
__ Go on a retreat
__ Spend Christmas in the desert
__ Stay for a month in an isolated cabin on a faraway lake
__ Spiritually comfort someone who is dying
__ Save a life
__ Witness a miracle
__ Write caring letters
__ Receive caring letters
__ Help the lowest of the low
__ See the joy radiate from someone's eyes

Sports

__ Be good at a sport
__ Snowboard or ski
__ Coach a sports team
__ Play a sport at the collegiate level
__ Play a sport at the professional level
__ Scuba dive
__ Learn to surf
__ Attend the Olympic games
__ Run a marathon
__ Use a trampoline
__ See a professional baseball game
__ See a professional soccer game
__ See a professional hockey game
__ See a rodeo
__ See the Harlem Globetrotters
__ Water ski
__ Try parachuting
__ Try rappelling
__ Bat against a professional baseball pitcher
__ Go hunting
__ Go fishing
__ See a bullfight
__ Steer a sailboat

Travel

__ Have dual citizenship
__ Cross the equator
__ Go on a cruise
__ Work on a ship
__ Travel frequently
__ Visit Transylvania
__ See the Danube River
__ Tour a European castle
__ Visit the tropics
__ Drive across the continent
__ Visit every continent
__ Walk from one continent into another
__ Visit all fifty states
__ Visit all ten Canadian provinces
__ Stroll on a sandy ocean beach at sunset
__ Drive on the Alaska Highway
__ Live and love in Vienna
__ Get lost in Venice
__ Visit New York
__ Visit Auschwitz
__ Visit Cape Town
__ Stand at Cape Agulhas, the southern tip of Africa
__ Sail through the Panama Canal
__ Cross the Mississippi River
__ Visit Texas
__ See Niagara Falls
__ Spend the summer in Côte d'Azur, Provence
__ Ride the Trans-Siberian Express
__ Study abroad
__ See the Rocky Mountains
__ See Mount Everest
__ Travel far with a friend
__ Walk the Appian Way in Rome
__ Travel aboard a freighter
__ Ride up front in a train
__ Travel alone on a train
__ See a desert
__ Be the most easterly or westerly person in a country
__ Stand in two countries at the same time
__ Return to your hometown
__ See where President Kennedy was assassinated
__ Visit a foreign embassy
__ See all the Great Lakes in one day

Life Experiences: Your Own Life

Here's your opportunity to start jotting down some of the things you've done in your life. On a separate sheet of paper, write down each of the experience categories from the above list. Then start adding experiences from your life.

After creating your list, you likely discovered many personal life experiences, each with a story to tell. Many of them, including "Careers, Jobs, and Work," "Family Matters," "Financial," "Health," and "Spiritual," mirror the legacy themes and can be used as memory prompts for new stories you had forgotten. Keep this list handy; it can lead to sudden inspiration and new ideas for stories. And remember that it serves as a memory jogger. Be sure to include those experiences unique to your life.

Appendix C: World Events Time Line

As the world spins on its axis, we hang on for the ride of our lives. All of us live within the framework of a much greater picture. We have survived a time line of several decades that includes major national and world events. Many of them have given context to our lives. Wars have disrupted our families. Economic devastation has torn some of us apart. Earthquakes, floods, and tornadoes have taken their toll. There are also moments of celebration—technological innovation, victory in sports, changes in government, and the coming of a new year. Each can play havoc with our best-laid plans. Each adds another twist to the day-to-day saga we call *life*.

There is a story for every year we live. It begins the year you were born and continues to the present time. It will reach into your future. You can place your life story events within this larger framework.

Many life stories are tempered by the Great Depression years. Others are colored by the turbulent cultural changes of the 1960s. As you write your themes, you can strengthen them by adding the context of the times in which they were experienced.

Look at the following world events time line. You will find that your history is also that of the world we live in.

World Events 1900—2015

1900–1910

1900 Kodak introduces one dollar Brownie camera
Second modern Olympic Games open in Paris

1901 Marconi sends radio broadcast over ocean
President McKinley assassinated

1902 Boer War ends

1903 Wright brothers' first flight
Ford Motor Company started

1904 Work starts on Panama Canal
Olympic Games in St. Louis, Missouri

1905 Theory of relativity published

1906 San Francisco earthquake
Mount Vesuvius erupts

1907 First electric washing machine

1908 Ford's Model T introduced
Boy Scouts started in U.K. by Baden-Powell

1909 Plastic invented

1910 Halley's Comet appears

1911–1920

1911 Mona Lisa stolen
Indianapolis 500 begins

1912 *RMS Titanic* sinks

1913 First crossword puzzle
Mona Lisa recovered

1914 WWI begins
Panama Canal opens
First traffic light

1915 Armenian genocide
RMS Lusitania sinks off Irish coast

1916 First self-serve grocery store opens in U.S.
Rasputin murdered

1917 Bolshevik Revolution in Russia
U.S. declares war on Germany

1918 Czar Nicholas II and family assassinated
WWI ends
Royal Air Force is founded

1919 Treaty of Versailles
Pop-up toaster invented

1920 Women get right to vote in U.S.

1921–1930

1921 Lie detector invented

1922 Insulin discovered

1923 *Time* magazine founded

1924 First Winter Olympic Games
Ellis Island closes as formal entry point

1925 Flapper dresses in style

1926 Robert Goddard fires his first liquid-fueled rocket

1927 Lindbergh flies nonstop from New York City to Paris
The Jazz Singer (first talkie film)

1928 Fleming discovers penicillin
Bubble gum invented

1929 Stock Market Crash
Car radio invented

1930 Pluto discovered
Mickey Mouse comic strip first published

1931–1940

1931 Empire State Building completed
First *Dracula* movie released

1932 Air conditioning invented
Sydney Harbor Bridge opens

1933 Hitler becomes Chancellor of Germany
FDR launches New Deal

1934 The Dust Bowl
Cheeseburger invented

1935 AA founded
Monopoly game goes on sale

1936 Spanish Civil War begins
Berlin Summer Olympic Games

1937 Hindenburg disaster
Nylon patented by DuPont

1938 Hitler annexes Austria
Dennis the Menace comic strip first published

1939 Spanish Civil War ends
WWII begins
Helicopter invented

1940 Battle of Britain
Trotsky assassinated

1941–1950

1941 Pearl Harbor
Jeep invented

1942 T-shirt introduced
Anne Frank goes into hiding

1943 Warsaw Ghetto Uprising

1944 Ballpoint pens go on sale
D-Day

1945 WWII ends
UN founded

1946 Bikinis introduced
Nuremberg Trial
"Iron Curtain" speech

1947 Dead Sea Scrolls discovered
Polaroid camera invented

1948 Berlin Airlift
Gandhi assassinated
Israel founded

1949 NATO established
China becomes communist

1950 Korean War begins
Peanuts comic strip first published
First modern credit card introduced

1951–1960

1951 UNIVAC I installed (first commercially available computer)
First color TV in U.S.

1952 Car seat belts introduced
Elizabeth becomes queen

1953 Mt. Everest climbed for first time
DNA discovered
Stalin dies
First *Playboy* magazine

1954 First atomic submarine launched
Report says cigarettes cause cancer

1955 Disneyland opens
Rosa Parks refuses to give up her bus seat

1956 Suez Crisis
Elvis on TV (rock 'n' roll era begins)
Hungarian Revolution

TV remote control invented

1957 Space Age begins

1958 Mao Zedong launches Great Leap Forward

Hula hoops become popular

1959 Castro becomes dictator of Cuba

Alaska and Hawaii become states

1960 Lasers invented

U-2 spy plane shot down over Soviet Union

1961–1970

1961 Berlin Wall

USSR puts first human in space

1962 Cuban Missile Crisis

1963 JFK assassinated

Profumo scandal in UK

1964 The Beatles appear on *The Ed Sullivan Show*

1965 U.S. sends troops to Vietnam

Watts riots in Los Angeles

1966 Star Trek airs

Chinese Cultural Revolution begins

1967 Canada's Centennial

Summer of Love

Six-Day War

1968 Martin Luther King assassinated

RFK assassinated

Tet Offensive in Vietnam

Prague Spring

1969 First moon landing

Woodstock

Sesame Street first airs

1970 Apollo 13

Kent State shootings

The Beatles break up

Computer floppy disks introduced

1971–1980

1971 VCR introduced

Pentagon Papers published

1972 Nixon visits China

Munich Olympics massacre

1973 Yom Kippur War

Salvador Allende overthrown in Chile

1974 Watergate—Nixon resigns

Patty Hearst kidnapped by SLA

1975 President Ford escapes assassination attempt

1976 Montreal Olympics

Jimmy Carter elected president

1977 Elvis Presley dies

TV miniseries *Roots* airs

Star Wars released

1978 First test-tube baby born

John Paul II becomes pope

1979 USSR invades Afghanistan

Three Mile Island nuclear incident

Iran hostage crisis begins

1980 Moscow Olympics

Ronald Reagan becomes U.S. President

John Lennon murdered

1981–1990

1981 Iran hostage crisis ends

AIDS first identified

IBM markets first Personal Computer (IBM PC)

1982 Falkland Islands invaded by Argentina
Michael Jackson releases "Thriller" LP

1983 Cabbage Patch dolls become popular
U.S. Embassy in Beirut bombed

1984 First Macintosh computer
Indira Gandhi assassinated
Bhopal poison gas leak

1985 Famine in Ethiopia
New Coke hits market
RMS Titanic wreck found

1986 *Challenger* shuttle explodes upon takeoff
Chernobyl accident

1987 DNA first used to convict criminals
Black Monday on New York Stock Exchange (NYSE)

1988 Pan Am Flight 103 bombed over Lockerbie
U.S. and Canada reach free trade agreement

1989 Tiananmen Square
Berlin Wall falls
Exxon Valdez spills millions of gallons of oil

1990 Lech Wałsa becomes first president of Poland
Nelson Mandela freed

1991–2000

1991 Operation Desert Storm in Persian Gulf
Collapse of the USSR

1992 Official end of the Cold War
Riots in L.A. after Rodney King verdict

1993 Waco massacre
World Trade Center bombed
Internet use grows exponentially

1994 Channel Tunnel opens
O.J. Simpson arrested for double murder
Rwandan genocide

1995 Oklahoma City bombing
Yitzhak Rabin assassinated

1996 Mad cow disease hits Britain
Unabomber arrested

1997 Princess Diana dies in car crash
Hong Kong returned to China
Scientists clone sheep

1998 India and Pakistan both test nuclear weapons
Viagra on the market
Titanic becomes most successful movie ever

1999 Euro becomes new European currency
Fear of Y2K bug
JFK Jr. dies in plane accident
NATO attacks Serbia

2000 USS Cole bombed
Unclear winner in U.S. presidential election
Mapping the human genome
Concorde crashes near Paris

2001–2010

2001 9/11 terrorist attacks in U.S.
Anthrax scare

Taliban regime in Afghanistan collapses

2002 Bali bombings

Moscow theatre hostage crisis

2003 Columbia shuttle explosion

Iraq War begins

2004 Indonesian tsunami

Madrid train bombings

Beslan school hostage crisis in Russia

George W. Bush reelected president

2005 Hurricane Katrina

Pope John Paul II dies

London terrorist bombings

2006 Saddam Hussein is convicted and hanged in Baghdad

Pluto is reclassified a dwarf planet

2007 Gordon Brown replaces Tony Blair as prime minister in U.K.

U.S. troop surge in Iraq War

2008 Cuban president Fidel Castro permanently steps down after 49 years in power

Barack Obama elected U.S. president

2009 US Airways Flight 1549 emergency landing in Hudson River

Michael Jackson dies

2010 Massive 7.0 earthquake hits Haiti

Explosion on BP oil rig causes largest marine oil spill in history

2011–CURRENT

2011 Japan 9.0 magnitude earthquake and tsunami lead to nuclear accident

Arab Spring

Osama bin Laden killed

2012 London Olympics

Hurricane Sandy

Encyclopedia Britannica ends print edition

Barack Obama reelected

2013 Pope Benedict XVI resigns

Pope Francis elected

Nelson Mandela dies

2014 Sochi Olympics

Russian Federation annexes Crimea

IFA World Cup in Brazil

Ebola crisis deepens

ISIS

2015 Lithuania establishes the euro as its official currency

Massacres continue in Nigeria by the Boko Haram group

Apple releases the iWatch

____

____

2016 ____________________

____

____

2017 ____________________

____

____

2018 ____________________

____

____

2019 ____________________

____

____

____

Many of these are international events that made the news, while others document moments in our technological and social evolution. Still others represent economic transformation. All of them can be used as frames for your life story time line. Were you born in 1948? The Berlin Airlift began that summer. Where were you on November 22, 1963 when President Kennedy was assassinated? Did you see The Beatles during their mid-1960s tours of the United States? The Iran hostage crisis began in 1979; did it have ramifications in your own life? The Cabbage Patch doll became a sensation in 1983; did you ever own one? Where were you living when the Berlin Wall fell in 1989? Did you have your own family then? Where did you work? In 1997 Princess Diana was killed. Do you remember who you were with when you heard the news? The memory of September 11, 2001 is indelible. We remember where we were and how we felt when the news came through: disbelief, anger, fear. Did you know someone who perished that morning? How did 9/11 change you? In 2012 President Obama won his second term. Were you excited or disappointed? Why?

We all own a share of history. Part of it is for us. When we write our life stories, they become part of the historical record.

Appendix D: Suggested Readings and Websites

Dozens of books and websites are dedicated to life story writing. We have selected those that are relevant to legacy writing. It's always a good idea to read up on the topic to gain additional perspectives. Using the suggested readings and websites can remind you that you aren't alone in this. Thousands of people are writing their life stories, and each day more resources become available.

Books

Courage and Craft: Writing Your Life into Story by Barbara Abercrombie

Writing the Memoir by Judith Barrington

Telling the Stories of Life Through Guided Autobiography Groups by James E. Birren and Kathryn N. Cochran

Braving the Fire: A Guide to Writing About Grief and Loss by Jessica Handler

Writing from Personal Experience: How to Turn Your Life into Salable Prose by Nancy Davidoff Kelton

The Power of Story by Jim Loehr

Remembering Your Story: Creating Your Own Spiritual Autobiography by Richard L. Morgan

The Power of Memoir: How to Write Your Healing Story by Linda Joy Myers

Memoirs of the Soul: A Writing Guide by Nan Merrick Phifer

Your Life as Story: Discovering the "New Autobiography" and Writing Memoir as Literature by Tristine Rainer

Writing Your Life: Putting Your Past on Paper by Lou Willett Stanek

LifeWriting: Drawing from Personal Experience to Create Features You Can Publish by Fred D. White

You Don't Have to Be Famous: How to Write Your Life Story by Steve Zousmer

Websites

Association of Personal Historians (APH): personalhistorians.org

The Birren Center for Autobiographical Studies: guidedautobiography.com

International Institute for Reminiscence and Life Review (IIRLR): 69.195.124.63/~reminis8

Life Story Library Foundation: lifestorylibrary.org

National Association of Memoir Writers (NAMW): namw.org

Writer's Digest: www.writersdigest.com

Bonus material for life story writing is available for download. You will find additional themes and exercises to assist you in your writing at www.guidedlifestories.com or www.guidedautobiography.com.

INDEX